ANIMATIONS

A TRILOGY FOR MABOU MINES

PERFORMING ARTS JOURNAL PUBLICATIONS
NEW YORK

LEE BREUER

EDITED BY **BONNIE MARRANCA** · **GAUTAM DASGUPTA**

Library of Congress Cataloging in Publication Data
Animations.
CONTENTS: Breuer, Lee. The Red Horse. The B.Beaver. The Shaggy Dog.
Library of Congress Catalog Card No.: 79-84185.
ISBN: 0-933826-01-X
ISBN: 0-933826-03-6(pbk)

Printed in the United States of America

Acknowledgement is made for permission to quote from the following:

Comte de Lautréamont, Maldoror, translated by Guy Wernham. Copyright 1943 by Guy Wernham. Reprinted by permission of New Directions.

Music for The Red Horse Animation. Copyright © 1968, 1971, 1979. Reprinted by permission.

Book Design: James Lapine
Graphic Design Assistants: Gautam Dasgupta, Eve Kessler, Art Presson
Typography: Publishers Typography Inc., Hicksville, New York
Printing: Lithocrafters, Chelsea, Michigan

TABLE OF CONTENTS

A SPECIAL DEDICATION TO:

SANDY S. AND KANDY C., PATRICK M., JACK T., SUZIE H., JOE B.
(IN MEMORIUM), TERRY O., LIBBUS T., RUSS M., BOB S., ERIN H.,
CAROLEE, CLETAGH YAZZI (IN MEMORIUM), LITTLE DOG, AND R.C.L.,
TURKEY, PARIS, L.A., N.Y.C., DEAD AND LIVING MUSES.

AUTHOR'S PREFACE

REALMS IS A WORK IN SIX PARTS . SIX LOKAS . SIX REALMS .
ARE SIX PLACES IN A MIND . SIX ILLUSIONS . HERE ARE
THREE . THE **ANIMATIONS** . THEY DEAL WITH ANIMALS .
GHOSTS . AND DEVILS . THREE MORE WILL DEAL WITH
GODS . HEROES . AND MEN . THEY WILL BE CALLED LIES . IT
IS TRADITIONALLY ASSUMED THAT UNLIGHTENED LIFE IS
LIVED IN THESE SIX REALMS IN ENDLESSLY VARYING
SEQUENCES ENDLESSLY REPEATED AND ENDLESSLY
RELIVED . I ACCEPT THIS TRADITIONAL ASSUMPTION MORE
READILY THAN OTHER TRADITIONAL ASSUMPTIONS SUCH AS
THE ONE THAT ASSUMES THAT LIFE IS LIVED IN THE EGO .
THE SUPEREGO . AND THE ID . OR THE ONE THAT ASSUMES
THAT LIFE IS LIVED IN THE BODY AND THE SOUL . OR THAT
LIFE IS LIVED IN PHILADELPHIA . THAT WAS W.C. FIELD'S
ASSUMPTION . IT IS ALSO ASSUMED THAT THIS ASSUMPTION
IS UNENLIGHTENED . THIS IS A STORY OF AN
UNENLIGHTENED LIFE .

INTRODUCTION

Looking over some notes I had made half a dozen years ago after an early viewing of THE RED HORSE ANIMATION I found this scribbling: "emotions are entirely formal." I didn't realize the implications of the remark at the time but after a few more years of seeing Mabou Mines perform the animations (RED HORSE, B.BEAVER, SHAGGY DOG) written for them by Lee Breuer in the period 1968-78, and reading the texts themselves, my initial comment seemed comprehensible in the context of the deeper structures of the trilogy. The texts began to make sense as Breuer's formalization of his own emotions.

It had always seemed disconcerting that the achievement of the animations as one of the major works of the American theatre in the seventies was based on the productions alone. As if the writing had no identity of its own apart from the productions. Breuer's direction of the animations, it is true, gave primacy to production values, and to some extent that choice has denied him his due as a writer.

In my Introduction to the comic book version of RED HORSE published in THE THEATRE OF IMAGES (Drama Book Specialists, 1977) I emphasized the work's performance aspects because it was my intention then to develop a performance vocabulary, not a poetics of narrative. Now I find it more compelling to look at the animations from a literary point of view, and to put aside temporarily Breuer's directorial conceptions to deal with him as a writer—to be more specific, to consider him as a playwright. The texts have a life of their own apart from their presentation in performance, and they can be read and enjoyed as literature—as plays. It is not my intention now to search for "a **7** meaning" in each animation but to uncover the multiplicity of meanings each work contains. In other words, to approach each animation in a way that embraces its unique sensuality in an equitable union of form and content: to highlight its structures of feeling. To the extent that the animations function on an autobiographical level, the area I want to focus on in this Introduction, Breuer-as-writer reveals his personal relationship to his art, and his feelings about being an artist.

Many artists draw all their resources from themselves and continually reflect only their own image. Breuer's use of autobiography, however, goes way beyond a purely narcissistic approach; he is self-projected, not self-centered. By that I mean he situates himself in a social context, and what he writes in his plays relates to the world around him. It is the I in "the world," not the "I" in its own world. If the animations can be said to treat consciousness from three different perspectives, and I believe that they can, what Breuer develops throughout them is a highly skillful thematics of consciousness.

He does this not through the projection of an omnipotent "I" but through the personalities of animals who, instead of people, are the principal "characters" in the plays. The notion of "animation" refers to the life spirit (the soul) he gives them. (Here it might be worth considering Roland Barthes's distinction between "figuration" and "representation" of the author in the text, the former based on presence, the latter on description.) Drawing on the rich and popular historical tradition of the beast epic Breuer creates his own fables of contemporary life and manners, telling us in his own punning fashion how the individual functions as a social "animal." These fables operate on at least two levels: metaphorically, they function as art about making art; mythically, they work to demystify stereotypical attitudes about malehood.

Breuer's choice of animals is not arbitrary, but works as a kind of totemic classification. The natural activities of each animal's (horse, beaver, dog) life are made to coincide with human modes of feeling and perception in the context of the plays. In this way, the horse evokes feelings of freedom and romance, the beaver creates defenses, and the dog is caught in a master/slave relationship. All of the latter are metaphors for certain intellectual and emotional positions, and are played with on several levels. And at the same time, from the mythic perspective Breuer debunks the male prerogative of knowing who you are. The metaphoric and mythic fuse and interact contrapuntally in the narrative line of the texts, with the metaphoric inviting a partly psychoanalytic approach, and the mythic the more structural.

By using metaphors of animals instead of an identifiable self Breuer distances himself from his material, allowing him to take an ironic stance toward it which he does every chance he gets. The result is literally a cross between the irony of Kafka's fables and the hyperbole of the animated cartoon, by Breuer's own admission the two most influential sources of the animation concept. The literary conceit of the fable gives him complete freedom of expression while at the same time offering the protection of a mask. Breuer has devised his texts in such a way that they show the "eye" looking at the "I." It is from this perspective that the animations reveal, not facts of life, but aspects of existence.

The use of autobiography, in the sense of the "self as text," is one of the characteristic features of current experimental theatre and performance art which in the seventies has been evolving new strategies for dealing with content. If theatre in the sixties was defined by the collaborative creation of the text, in recent years individual authorship has gained ascendancy; likewise, theatre in the sixties (and all offshoots of the Happenings, too) was outer-directed whereas now it (and performance art) is inner-directed: perhaps the shift can be said to be from the exploration of environmental space to the exploration of mental space, and from narration to documentation. Following the current interest in America in a highly refined spiritual life and the evolution of new shapes of consciousness, the performing arts are actively redefining their own spirit: in both cases, the emphasis is on the dialogue with the self.

The animations, in particular, show a conscious development of personal mythology, a tendency to be found in the plays of Richard Foreman and Spalding Gray, and the operas of Meredith Monk, just to name a few examples. It seems more than coincidental that both Breuer and Gray refer to their work under the title of "trilogy" and that Foreman has evolved a "cycle" of plays with the same themes and characters. In my view this terminology reflects the authors' decided attempts to develop continuing self-histories—a fact which is not surprising because Americans have always defined themselves as individuals, not as a society or group.

In a larger context Breuer seems to be following the mythopoeic strain in the American avant-garde (some examples: The Living Theatre, The Open Theater, Robert Wilson); for the seventies I think we can redefine this strain as "auto-mythopoeic." The Romantic self is very much evident in Breuer's animations and Breuer, whose oeuvre is based on the life of the spirit, is the most expressionistic, poetic (and literary) of his contemporaries. The animations are Breuer's memory of the past (documentary time) related in the present (narrative time), the temporal narrative lines fusing in a self-conscious consciousness. ANIMATIONS continues the American tradition of transcendentalism.

Breuer animates his work with his own life spirit, the deepest part of his being. The part Charles Olson called the poet's "breath." It is this breath which gives life to the animals, and "animates" them so that they "become" human. Then Breuer's literary imagination takes over, letting all his feelings and perceptions loose in an idiosyncratic stream of consciousness that reflects a funky speechifying animal double. In this universe of words that each animal creates, poetry does its dance as a humorous intelligence. Caution: Breuer dances with two left feet.

Breuer's fables are poems for pleasure; entertaining, intelligent, sensual, they are the work of a master ironist. Not to mention a closet esoteric-type who delights in pedagogical humor. In passage after passage of virtuosic uses of metaphors and metonymy, rhetorical devices, macaronic verse, neologisms, sound rhythms, and free associations on verbal and visual ideas, Breuer creates quite dazzling poetry. The animations develop a metalanguage that seems to make itself up as it goes along, surprisingly rich in its imaginative devices and lack of regularity. It is writing about writing. Breuer especially loves language in the context of the speech act. No wonder the animals are all compulsive talkers, forever going on about themselves. By telling their stories, they situate themselves in the world.—"I speak therefore I am." The trilogy is really based on the art of storytelling, a vanishing form in the technological age which, as Walter Benjamin lamented, has substituted mere information-giving for "the ability to exchange experiences." (With what foresight Benjamin prophesied the information-giving nature of contemporary art!)

Breuer's intention is precisely that—to offer experience in the subtle form of corrective comedy. It is not surprising then that his work takes the form of the aphorism so often; the aphoristic style lends itself to offering advice, relating a moral, or commenting satirically with the intent to inform. Breuer's pithy remarks on the state of human affairs are all the more comical coming from the mouths of animals who appear hopelessly and helplessly human in their predicaments. (Like Kafka's mouse Josephine fussing about the relationship of her art to her audience.)

And what wonderfully intelligent creatures these animals are, with their liberated word play, delight in crisscrossing verbal and visual puns, and witty circumlocution. The puns, especially, emphasize the circularity of speech, the result being that ideas and images can be extended virtually infinitely, the verbal interacting with the visual not only in pure madcap fun, but often in highly sophisticated associations. Robert Pincus-Witten identifies a California sensibility in the proclivity toward punning, a fact which is not far-fetched when one considers that Breuer grew up in California and keeps in touch with the West Coast scene. In a more personal vein, he reflects the laid back tone of Californians and their playful attitude toward art and artifacts. The pun is the most dominant rhetorical device in the animations.

From a dramatic point of view the most distinctive aspect of the animations is the complete lack of dialogue. Even though other figures may appear (B.BEAVER, SHAGGY DOG) or be referred to (RED HORSE) in the plays, neither discourse nor conflict between characters is dramatized at any time in performance; that is to say, performers do not relate to each other in performance. Think for a moment about the implications of a drama that doesn't dramatize anything: it means that the dramatization of a conflict on stage, the conventional (and even unconventional) definition of drama is completely undermined. My own feeling is that the continued emphasis on the life of the spirit (the holistic approach to life, the integrated personality) and the turning away from rationalist thought may lead us in time—though not the foreseeable future—to a drama which is not based on conflict. Breuer's animations are the touch of a suggestion of this direction.

Breuer's radical conception of dramaturgy disregards the conventional uses of plot, dialogue, setting, time, and character in favor of an open-ended form that has the shape of the prose poem. The idea of passages in a life is substituted for plot, in place of dialogue he puts the monologue, instead of setting he develops the notion of personal space, memory takes over for dramatic time and, as I have already pointed out, the chorus takes the place of the individual character.

Breuer's use of chorus is not thematic or information-giving, as is usually the case, but works as the structural backbone of the animation, reflecting his conception of character in the drama: polyphonic voices substitute for the individual voice. Through the device of the chorus the narration evolves from several perspectives in the metonymic functioning of the actors; the notion of gender doesn't exist, nor does any separation between the past and the present. And, as in Oriental theatre, the voice is separated from the character. The actors as it were take turns enacting events from the animal's life rather than imitating them. Interestingly, Peter Handke's "Sprechstücke" also feature choruses ("speakers") instead of individuated characters, a musical approach to text, literary ready-mades, and lack of dialogue. But the important difference between Breuer and Handke is that the latter creates works which have no visual orientation, while Breuer is interested in motivational acting (the emotive gesture) in highly imagistic settings. Notwithstanding, Breuer and Handke share the distinction of having created a few of the most provocative texts for the stage in the last decade.

Yet, the animations are as free-flowing and personal as the "Sprechstücke" are schematic and objective. The poetic monologues that comprise the animations lend themselves to expressivity because they are temporarily unrestricted. The monologue seems to work for Breuer as the natural organizer of his lyrical outpourings. From the perspective of autobiography, the monologues function as mediators of the unconscious. If as Jacques Lacan observes, "the unconscious is the discourse of the Other," then it is the place where Breuer talks to himself.

Though the monologue is the unifying structure of the plays, Breuer relates his fables in a variety of ways. His is not story theatre, however, which is illustrative, but epic theatre, a dialectical one. Extending Bertolt Brecht's ideas about epic acting, the chorus, the autonomy of each theatrical element, and the narrative aspect of the performing space itself, Breuer tells his stories not only literally but musically, filmically, electronically, sculpturally, spatially, diagrammatically, kinetically, photographically, chromatically (not always in the same animation, of course)—all of them functioning as different and autonomous kinds of "writing" in the grammar of the event. Breuer refers to this technique as "tracking": it simply means the laying down of parallel lines of narration. In this way, the background and all elements of staging comment on what the performers, who theatricalize states of being, say and do. In Breuer's narrative strategy all space is semantic; everything in it emphasizes its conception as "writing."

These approaches to narrative link Breuer no doubt with Brechtian aesthetics, but there are other theatrical parallels as well. Perhaps the most obvious influence is Samuel Beckett (by way of James Joyce) whose use of narrative and the monologue, and treatment of consciousness, is unmistakably a presence in the animations. (Breuer's understanding of Beckett is fiercely evident in his brilliant stagings of PLAY, COME AND GO, and THE LOST ONES.) One can also see affinities with the work of Gertrude Stein, particularly her emphasis on consciousness and the continous present, the lack of dialogue, stage directions and individualized characters in her plays, and the announcement of sections of a play within the play itself. This aphorism of Stein's seems profoundly descriptive of the formal arrangement of Breuer's plays on the page: "A sentence is not emotional, a paragraph is."

In a more contemporary American context, Breuer aligns himself with the poets' theatre of Frank O'Hara and Kenneth Koch in their integration of art theories in drama, and the mixing of popular and classical literary forms; theirs, however, is a much more literary approach to theatre than Breuer's. Closer to Breuer's own manipulation of language is that of Sam Shepard; both writers love to play with the "attitude" in various styles of American vernacular speech. Coincidentally, the two (characteristically "California" artists) reflect the liberated poetic style of the Beats, their romanticism and their interest in musicalizing literary texts.

These theatrical and dramatic lines, and modern literary tradition appear side by side with the strong currents from the art world which inform the animations. From RED HORSE to B.BEAVER to SHAGGY DOG one can trace, respectively, a movement from minimalism to process art to super-realism in the execution of the texts. They also connect with the emotional attitude of abstract expressionism (isn't that a style that makes emotion "formal"?), pop art, and the more recent story art

(John Baldessari, Bill Beckley, William Wegman), and to a greater extent, the punning and ready-made concepts that descend from Marcel Duchamp, and which are refashioned in the more contemporaneous art of Robert Rauschenberg, Jasper Johns, and Bruce Nauman. Finally, and not the least important, as a sophisticated conceptual theatre Mabou Mines has a long history of collaborating with artists on their productions (Tina Girouard, Jene Highstein, Gordon Matta-Clark); no other theatre group in America can make this claim. (An odd contradiction in Mabou Mines' position vis-à-vis the art world is the fact that while the group is so art-oriented, art world people haven't given them full recognition because they tend to dislike the attempt to use trained performers, preferring instead the untrained.)

What is remarkable about the creation of the animations is their ability to accommodate the most contemporary styles of art with theatrical history and literary tradition, in a form derived from the cartoon! Breuer is among the very few gifted playwriting talents in the post-absurdist theatre. That is quite startling when one considers that he is generally thought of as a director rather than as a playwright, nor are the animations seriously talked about as plays—by the press or the public.

Before moving on to more detailed observations of each animation, I'd like to make some brief remarks about the way the texts are published in this volume for which we have tried to develop a new approach to documentation of texts. Lee Breuer (with the help of designer James Lapine) devised an original concept for the layout of each animation that would express its individuality as a text while at the same time suggesting how it looked in performance. One of the pleasures in reading ANIMATIONS is following the typographical uniqueness of each play, seeing how each play "thinks."

The dynamism of the texts is captured in capitalization, bold-face type, and the design of certain words or phrases to suggest moods, attitudes, and thematic or structural significance, such as the stutter letters in B.BEAVER and SHAGGY DOG's "chapter" headings. Overall there is a high iconic quality which reinforces the texts' appearance as poetry, and Breuer's position as an imaginative writer whose writing has a life of its own on the page. It is the kind of writing that incorporates its own written signs as an idiosyncratic grammar.

14 The intrusion of the photographs from the performance as "inter-texts" makes reading the animations more than a literary experience; one can read the rhetoric of the images, too. Together, then, the text and image interact in a sophisticated performance of their own—the text is theatricalized—relating not on a simple analogical basis but each supplying information the other cannot. Those free spaces which appear where there are no photographs allow the reader time to dream as it were, just as the filled-in (photographic) spaces which "quote" scenes from the performance, allow time to think beyond or along with the image. The "meaning" rests between the text and the image. This gives the reader a creative role in the "making" of the animations, since he must situate himself somewhere between the text and the performance to make the provocative transference between the literal and the metaphorical. The emphasis then shifts from the text to the reader.

Alternating the vertical and horizontal placement of text and photograph creates a challenging dialectic, and transvalues the notion of caption as well. These texts, based on the comic which has been traditionally considered a "low" art form, give the comic book literary respectability, but more to the point, they extend its formal and narrative possibilities while retaining its essential visual idea.

■

The first play of the trilogy, THE RED HORSE ANIMATION, is a romance which offers an outline of a narrative, not a complete story, in a tripartite structure: outline, lifeline, storyline. The different lines are not exactly structurally harmonic, but three related approaches to the play. The outline, however, remains the structural basis of RED HORSE, and the lifeline and storyline merge after its prologue.

The story purposely fragments the sense of time beginning as the play itself acknowledges, somewhere in the middle. As a narrative mode which derives its aesthetic from the comic book, it clearly tries to "frame" (to arrest) certain moments in the horse's life, without constructing a chronological order. The first third of the play is a taped prologue which suggests the words of a narrator talking out loud as if in a daydream, but when the actors enter the performing space at its conclusion, they take over as both the metaphoric and anthropomorphic image of a horse. They perform the piece for the most part lying down on the performing space which, in painting terms, refers to a canvas, and to extend the allusion further, aligns itself with the abstract expressionist technique of emotionalizing space—the process I referred to earlier as Breuer's formalization of his own emotions.

When the actors take over after the ''voice'' grows silent, they evolve a choral narrative, each one speaking for the horse. This choral structure reflects the division into three parts of what is really the interior monologue of the only ''character'' in RED HORSE, the most isolated, inner-directed world—and the most Beckettian in its intense study of consciousness—depicted in the animations. The play follows the logic of the dream world where the narrator and his idea of a horse become a unified being expressing real emotions. When this happens the outline begins to animate itself.

ROMAN NUMERAL TWO . IN WHICH I THINK I SEE MY SHAPE . This desire to know the landscape of his body—in the sense of both physical and mental terrain—is the compulsive drive of the horse in this journey play of sorts. The narration of the play is linked to the recognition of form so much so that it is spatially organized, developing in its movement a definable geometry of emotion. Form, shape, circle, line: these are the repeated terms of the horse's attempt to trace himself in space. (Coincidentally, these forms reflect the iconic vocabulary of minimalism which has strongly influenced this work in its technical approach.) In the emotional world of RED HORSE space functions in the form of codes for actual states of being. A circle, therefore, isn't simply a roundness but has to do with circularity in the ontological sense.

When the narrator in the prologue talks about diagramming an outline in blue pencil he draws a knot; with a red pencil he draws a line between some numbers and the shape of a horse appears. Reflecting on his spirit he sees a map, he starts ''mapping'' consciousness. Now the significance of the play's spatial organization becomes clearer. Travel and distance function not only as literal ideas, but as symbolic and psychological codes, too. (Travel as a journey to ''inner space'' and in the sense of covering ''aesthetic'' distance.) When the horse begins to construct a history of himself, he evolves a topography of the spirit.

In an autobiographical context, the obsession with form suggests that the narrator is struggling to discover his identity and style as an artist.

16 I'M CHANGING . WHAT AM I . The theme is intricately woven, on the one hand, with the metaphor of freedom and adventure the horse represents and, on the other, with the horse's domestication. These conflicting feelings are purposefully confused in parts of the story but coalesce in a dream sequence which features a scene between father and son. The idea of RED HORSE is that it is about fragmentation and contradictory feelings even as it evolves, if only temporarily, as a romance.

The story seems to me full of indecision, ambiguity, doubt, reversing of positions and the sense of impermanence; so much of the intensity of its "presentness" has to do with its singular focus of an artist, somewhat anguished, trying to find himself yet still having a sense of humor about it (if only as a defensive measure). RED HORSE does not develop a singular dramatic line (it has three) but offers a variety of narrative approaches in addition to the spatial narration. The story is also told filmically, diagrammatically, musically, metaphorically, chromatically. These different narrative modes do not always synthesize but work in counterpoint, as do the play's themes and images, in a deliberate discontinuity of codes.

DO I OWE A DEBT TO THE CINEMA? the horse asks (Capital Letter A), wondering about what may have influenced him; at the same time RED HORSE itself "thinks" filmically. ELEVEN . SEVEN . GENGHIS KHAN INSTITUTES THE CRAFT OF DELIVERY . BY HORSE . CUT . PAN OF THE GOBI DESERT . CUT . The "film" depicts the romance of a Mongolian steed, simultaneously uniting the narrator's romantic childhood memory of a film shown in grade school and his subconscious adult feelings about losing his freedom (being domesticated). The horse image has both positive and negative denotations which carry conflicting iconic and symbolic messages.

The horse undergoes a further symbolic transformation in the section which appears as the exposition of a conflict between father and son. One of the more lyrical passages of RED HORSE, this section finds the horse looking at his reflection in a stream—a pun on the "stream of consciousness"—and remembering his father, Daily Bread, in a dream that flashes by like a movie in his head. One of the reasons why Breuer's autobiographical writings don't remain at the solipsistic level —this scene especially demonstrates why—is his ability to objectify himself: the horse looks at himself in the stream and a third self looks at the horse looking at the reflection. At the core of the dream, and here the horse experiences an epiphany, is the horse's disapproval of his father's obsession with work and making money; the rejection of a bourgeois life style (his father's "domestication") in favor of the bohemian insecurity of an artistic one (his own). If Daily Bread was into "bread" (money) and "circles" (treadmill of success), his son is into "lines." But in which direction do they point? And what are they saying? In the pastoral setting of RED HORSE (B.BEAVER and SHAGGY DOG are urban pieces) the scene is almost elegiac.

If the romance is the traditional form for the wish-fulfillment dream, Breuer subverts the logic of its conventions so that it works in opposition to the outcome of the play. The horse never finds a form he can hold onto but wanders frustrated, goes back to the beginning of the story, and finally loses his sense of self. DON'T KNOW WHAT TO CALL ROMAN NUMERAL SIX . At the end of the story the horse can no longer keep himself together and his image begins to fall apart into space. The narrator's dream is over, and the grim realities of self-doubt come crashing through the frame. THE RED HORSE ANIMATION is Breuer's most poetic, subdued, and reflective work.

■

In his second animation Breuer introduces B.Beaver, a Job-like figure struggling to build a dam which will secure his house and family. He HAS LOST THE ART OF DAMNATION AT A CRUCIAL TIME B.Beaver tells, in his six-chapter story which moves from the statement of his problem to its resolution. While RED HORSE exists wholly in the mind of the horse, B.BEAVER recounts the past; and, unlike the brooding horse, the beaver is a compulsive, stuttering cartoon, the most comical of Breuer's creations.

As published here, the story is divided into "text" and "takes." The text is the actual narrative by B.Beaver who acts as a chorus leader while the others he refers to (the brood and the missus) function as a chorus; but whether they are the beaver's mental projections or real family members is not clarified in the text—the beaver is telling his own story. The chorus amplifies aural and visual images of the text with the takes serving as Breuer-as-writer's self-conscious comments on it. The text relates to the past, the takes to the present. The "I" of the story is seen from the perspective of "he" in the takes.

These takes are introduced into the story as literary allusion (B.Beaver

18 is aligned with another comic TURD in dramatic history—Ubu Roi), pop allusion (to the animated cartoon voice of M. MAGOO), free association (on LATIN as related to language and a Puerto Rican social club), cartoon and visual cues (THE DAM COLLAPSES . CURTAINS FLAIL . YIKES . EXPLODES ACROSS THE FRAME .); the text serves to detail character and interpret mood and attitude, too (the last take goofs on the clichés of a sentimental soundtrack).

This emphasis on process has greater significance in the thematic organization of the play itself; in fact, it is its subject. B.BEAVER is a story about not being able to write, or, being afraid to let writing happen. It is a metaphoric explication on the theme of "writer's block," cleverly disguised in a hilarious story whose lovable hero is a beaver trying to construct a dam (a defense mechanism) so he and his family won't wash away when the snow melts in the spring. (Perhaps I understood this on a purely subconscious level since I was going through the same thing at the time I was beginning to work on this Introduction.) B.Beaver stutters for a very good reason—he can't get the words out. Stuttering is emblematic of his creative problems. In the punning universe that defines B.BEAVER, you're "damned" if you do, "dammed" if you don't.

The beaver creates all sorts of distractions to deny his creative urge. He gets sidetracked on pedagogical thoughts about geological formations, writes a postcard with a request for "how to" books on building dams; floating downstream he daydreams happy thoughts of escape, twirling his tail around a tree branch he hangs upside down contemplating his dilemma. In one of his fantasies he finds a waterlogged craft and pretends he is captain of a ship, mixing nautical and boxing language for a pun on the idea of creativity. B.Beaver has his serious moments, too; swimming past some workers along the brook bank, he observes: LOOK AT THEM ... EAT . CRAP . SCREW . CROAK. He refuses "death on the installment plan."

The observation has more than pictorial ramifications because it expands upon the important section from RED HORSE which explores the philosophical differences of father and son. Here again in the second part of the trilogy the opposition to the banality of the workaday world surfaces. It seems to me that the narrator hasn't resolved the conflict between wanting security for his family, but not wanting to trade the insecurity of the artist's life for a dreary bourgeois life-style. Though family-centered plays have traditionally dominated American drama, this has not been the case in experimental theatre. An exception to this generalization is the animations which feature as an important theme the acceptance of parental responsibility: central to the trilogy is the conflict between a writer wanting to feel free to follow his creative impulses while at the same time wanting to fulfill his responsibilities as a father. As subject matter in an avant-garde context this is pretty rare. (On the other hand, that Breuer is one of the few people in the avant-garde theatre who has a family easily accounts for his concerns.) Not surprisingly, two of the animals he chooses to tell his stories are "domesticated" (horse and dog), the third is involved in defending his home (beaver).

If on the metaphorical level B.BEAVER acts as a fable about the artist, on the mythical level it demolishes myths about the male "animal" in society. The beaver is continually constructing defenses, and experiencing anxiety and fear about his impulses. He is hiding behind the dam and the desire to keep his family together, afraid of his own creative responses to the world around him. Breuer distorts the portrait of the artist as a confident young man conquering new creative territory for himself.

The story of the uptight beaver is told in a variety of ways that mix Latin, naval language, and clichés with the argot of sports, science, meteorology, algebra, and biology. The different kinds of speech express the frequent transformations in states of mind experienced by the beaver. The imagery, too, reinforces the play's psychological themes.

The most obvious symbol is the dam which, stationary, holds back the creative flow and, washed away, lets creativity come gushing forth. There are other images more tied to nature which, in the deeper structure of the story, become a metaphor for artistic struggle as one of survival against the elements (the beaver hunts salmon instead of the white whale, though). The snow, this massive pure blankness, is a "block" which when thawed will let the creative juices flow, while water itself is the temporary setting for the beaver's floating dreams. In the scheme of things is it any wonder that after the winter and with the coming of spring, the beaver makes his breakthrough? Breuer's use of symbols rests fairly traditionally in his radically-conceived play.

One of the joys of Breuer's writing is its sensual quality. SHAGGY DOG is

20 the animation about sexual attitudes, but B.BEAVER has its own special erotics. When the beaver is finally on the verge of accepting his creative impulses he grows excited sexually and has an erection: he prepares "to come" into his own as an artist. In this way writing is associated with orgasm on the physiological level, and with the building of a structure, on the physical. (Regarding this last point, the notion of creating art as making a work—physical labor—is very much in the vocabulary of contemporary artists in all fields, as if they feel the need, as Americans in a country which values manual labor and devalues artistic labor, to justify their activities as work.)

In THE B.BEAVER ANIMATION Breuer has created a very sophisticated cartoon about being a writer: a genuinely funny, self-effacing work that proves how unpretentious an artist Breuer is. The sort who would stub his toe on a statue of the muse. Breuer's witty union of sexual and intellectual humor in exaggerated settings construed to emphasize human foibles make him the Groucho Marx of the American avant-garde.

■

Breuer's gifts as an imaginative writer create a striking presence in THE SHAGGY DOG ANIMATION. Now, in this animation, five times longer than any other, he creates the space for his soul to sing. The voice belongs to a dog called Rose, and sing she does—a torch song about her man that got away. The story of a filmmaker/dog Rose, SHAGGY DOG is a bittersweet soap opera with a cast of characters who include, besides Rose and another dog Broadway, a rabbit, Bunny, and two humans, John and Leslie, all of whom appear in a series of adventures that unravel in California, Las Vegas, and New York. It is a love story that makes fun of love, mocking its illusions, pain, sentimentality and foolishness, while acknowledging its supreme ecstasy. Sounds like the definition of "puppy love."

SHAGGY DOG is all reflecting surfaces, electronic perfection, artificial emotion: romance as fabricated in movies and sung about in popular songs. To get at the craziness of his subject Breuer musicalizes the text in performance, using different kinds of musical styles for the "attitude" they embody, so that SHAGGY DOG becomes at times talking rock, with all sound filtered through the sophisticated stereophonic equipment that manipulates the voices of nine performers who speak for Rose in solo, trio, and choral form. I don't wish to deal with performance per se—that's not my focus here—but it is necessary to know the basic set-up of the play to understand Breuer's canny remark to an interviewer: "You can't say 'I love you' anymore without an echo chamber...[it] has captured the myth of the expression more clearly than the human voice." Music so dominates contemporary notions of romance that people identify experience with the musical theme it suggests to them. Rose tells John in her special idiolect: HOW LONG . HAD I LONGED . TO SING THE SONG . THAT PLUGGED YOUR PRONG . INTO MY SOCKET . AND THERE IT WAS . SWEETS . KINKY REGGAE .

SHAGGY DOG is the perfect piece for the disco age. Slick, controlled, stylish, and synthetic. It has to do with performance: in the sense of the performing self, and in relation to definitions of metatheatre. In the world Breuer creates characters act out ideal romantic images of themselves in a glossy setting decorated with the gadgetry of a technological society. Never mind a Saturday night fever, Rose is in heat.

The play's slickness characterizes avant-garde theatre now, as opposed to ten years ago when technology wasn't so prominent in it, and the more advanced theatre had a homemade, "poor" quality. SHAGGY DOG is "rich" in more ways than one: it represents more sophisticated theatrical conceptualization as well as more money available for experimentation. The movement from RED HORSE (minimalism) to SHAGGY DOG (post-minimalism) has been to progressively more color and technological equipment. In SHAGGY DOG style is subject.

A "Love Story" for the avant-garde, SHAGGY DOG is based entirely on the clichés of romance as it is depicted in popular mythology, and propagated by the mass media. When Rose and John make love on a California beach A WAKI LUA LANI KALOA KALUA MOON surfs over them; John (a filmmaker himself) creates cinematic illusions of his affairs with Leslie (I REMEMBER ONCE PROJECTING A PLACE IN THE SUN ONTO LESLIE). Not only are there puns on and allusions to songs and film (these are used throughout the production), but to television (Kojak is on Rose's "telly") and to consumer products (A HOBART 700 SPEED QUEEN DISHWASHER sits in her kitchen). It's the innocence of pop art updated in the detached cool of super-realism: a "California" (in sensibility and in place) love story according to pop culture.

SHAGGY DOG takes the form of an extended "Dear John" letter from the narrator Rose (a puppet as well as a dog) to John (her owner) in which she reflects on their relationship which ended three years ago (twenty-one in the dog's cycle). It works itself out in a binary structure of "sound track" in which the actual narrative unfolds (the subjective line) and "image track" in which the text comments on itself (the objective line), the two tracks together evolving as a fugue.

The story itself is basically very simple though it takes an incredibly circumlocuitous path to its unraveling—it is a shaggy dog story: prologue (a kind of radio play which takes place before the image track appears in the text); Part I in which Rose recalls the high points of her love affair; Part II in which John and Rose break up; Part III, three years after the affair. The animation follows virtually a classical narrative line: a heroine comes to know the truth about herself by going through a series of meaningful experiences. Of course, these experiences are not dramatized, only recalled by Rose.

In essence, Rose moves from feeling I WAS THE DIMENSION OF THE SHADOWY SPACE FROM ONE SHOE TO ANOTHER (her first meeting with John) to MY LIFE HAS CHANGED . IT'S TAKEN A TRULY INWARD TURN . MY FEELINGS HAVE BECOME THE FACTS . . . AND OUTSIDE I FELT SO PROFOUND I CONTROLLED THE WEATHER (Rose has an epiphany in the snow) to GOODBYE . DEAR . I SAID . AND SANK INTO THE NIGHT LIKE A PIECE OF BACON IN THE BOWL OF SPLIT PEA SOUP (the corny simile wonderfully props up Rose's cool resolve to go her own way). By the last few pages of the play Rose has become fully militant, quoting Lautréamont's MALDOROR in a passage about dogs who break their chains and run madly through the countryside, unable to control their new-found freedom. SHAGGY DOG traces the movement of the soul toward liberation; in Rose's case, the development of a feminist consciousness.

A work I don't think would have been possible without the influence of the women's movement, SHAGGY DOG is a mature feminist statement of remarkable metaphoric and philosophic richness. It demonstrates the awakening of consciousness in a series of ironic events that are both humorous and profoundly moving and, even more significant, it reflects a movement away from the more self-absorbed earlier animations to a much broader social context.

Yet, there is much more to SHAGGY DOG than the contemporaneity of its feminism. As an artist Rose acts as a metaphor for Breuer's own feelings about being an artist. But she is also a puppet, physically manipulated in performance by performers (male and female) who are in turn manipulated by a sound system, a concrete allusion to her emotional manipulation by John (the image track studies the problem as it relates to the MECHANISM OF ATTACHMENT). As an abstract idea the puppet refers to the aesthetics of Bunraku which is an art based on the idea of storytelling through music, and furthermore, a theatrical mode which separates the narration into three separate "tracks" as it were: singer, puppet, manipulators.

And just as Rrose (a Rose is a Rose is a Rose) Selavy represents Duchamp's feminine nature (even as a name "Rose" has mythological status), so she is emblematic of the narrator's view as expressed in the clichés of an oppressed minority, a view encompassing both androgyny and metamorphosis. This very special Rose is a dog owned by a master—the metaphor for the narrator's perception of the artist enslaved (owned by) the art world. Metaphor is clearly the organizing principle of the animations, more complexly in SHAGGY DOG than the others, because here metaphors are doubled in Rose's status as both dog and artist.

The real coup of SHAGGY DOG is that Rose is so believable as a human being and artist, in a narrative that offers the multiple perspectives of the "I" who tells the story and the "they" who comment on it without involving them as writers. The irony of the image track keeps the reader from falling into the sentimentality that the story is constantly bouncing off of in the sound track. To make matters more complicated in this already beautifully complicated story, there is also a film metaphor to suggest that SHAGGY DOG is a movie that John and Rose are separately evolving in their heads. John (a shooter) and Rose (a cutter) get confused as to who's in who's scenario. Early on in the story Rose comments: ME AND MY MOVIE . WE WENT INTO PRODUCTION . ALL MY LINES CAME TRUE It came together for Rose and John in Venice. With Leslie off making a commercial, they wander off to the beach, make love and dream in a scene which depicts the most total convergence of animal and human species in the animations. Here is a sample of Rose's poetry:

WE'LL PICK UP DISEASES . AND FOAM AT THE MOUTH AND GET THIN AND CIVILIZED LIFE WILL SHUN OUR KIND . THEY'LL CALL OUT THE CATCHERS . BUT WE'LL ESCAPE . PAST SANTA BARBARA . PAST SAN LUIS OBISBO . PAST GORDA . SPECIAL PEOPLE WILL AID AND ABET US . ROMANTIC PEOPLE . THEY'LL BLOW KISSES FROM SPORTS CARS AND BECKON US TO THEIR BEACH BLANKETS WHERE THEY'LL TOAST OUR HEALTH IN A TEQUILA SUNRISE RIGHT OUT OF A THERMOS .

24 This passage includes all of the most characteristic features of the
animation in general: clichés of popular romance, parodistic humor and
imagery, motifs of Romanticism, California sensibility, poetic language,
fantasy.

Alas, back in civilization love starts to fade and Rose and John drift
apart. Sick with grief Rose overeats, throws temper tantrums when
John is with Leslie, takes a new lover, Bunny—all of the things humans
do to compensate for a broken heart. But by the end of Part II Rose no
longer needs John and she leaves him on a New York street at 4:00
a.m. while they're out for a walk. Rose is liberated, now it's John's turn
to suffer. Breuer creates a tour de force scene in Part III which shows
a distraught John, now a ''puppet'' himself, simultaneously dialing
John's Anonymous and a girlfriend:

> WHAT CAN I DO . I GO INTO MYSELF . I BECOME SELF INVOLVED . I TRY TO BE SELF
> EFFACING . BUT THAT'S SELF DEFEATING . I INDULGE IN SELF RECRIMINATION . BUT
> ALL THAT DOES IS MAKE ME MORE SELF CENTERED .

Breuer is relentless in this satirical ''closeup'' of John which makes fun
of current self-help jargon and reverses the position of the male in the
relationship. Meanwhile, Rose is on the sound track admitting that she
misses John: even with age (Rose is now twenty-one years older) one
never loses illusions about love. SING ME A CHORUS OF CHERRY PIE ... I TELL YOU
THE TRUTH . ONLY SLEEPING DOGS LIE . Rose ends SHAGGY DOG quoting a song
and a cliché —the twin foundations of a love relationship.

SHAGGY DOG evolves a style which I think of as ''Quotation Art'':
bolstered by the ironic stance of the artist it is a way of creating art
from the clichés and conventions embodied in the intellectual and
emotional patterns of a given society. Quotation Art embraces the
literary ready-made, a narrative strategy not without its striking
examples here and in Europe. Peter Handke's ''Sprechstücke'' come
readily to mind with Robert Wilson's A LETTER FOR QUEEN VICTORIA which
took much of its language, not from officialese, maxims, slogans, and
advertisements as Handke did, but from television programming, and
Sam Shepard's TOOTH OF CRIME whose dialogue is filled with the argot of
the rock, sports, crime, and business worlds. In each of these
examples artists have taken the vernacular of their society and turned
it back on itself—Handke for political purposes; Breuer, Wilson, and

Shepard for more mythic strategies. The idea of Quotation Art is that it is an art rooted in signs: it moves all imagery and language in multiple directions, with the signifier continually becoming the signified. SHAGGY DOG transmits Breuer's ideas about the ways in which the individual is socialized (programmed) by his/her internalization of popular mythology in a series of different codes (aural, symbolic, iconic, musical, linguistic, etc.) by which culture functions as a language.

Claude Lévi-Strauss's definition of the creation of myth from the "remains and debris of events . . . odds and ends . . . fossilized evidence of the history of an individual or a society" is provocative in this context. Mythical thought as "an intellectual form of 'bricolage.' " If anything, Breuer's quotation of certain American mythologies is a recycling of the junk of an advanced technological society to create a form which acts as a critique of that society. SHAGGY DOG is love among the ruins.

SHAGGY DOG works at the level of critique because it satirizes, instead of simply mocking, popular culture, a position which reinforces its moral underpinning. (Conversely, Theatre of the Ridiculous, a style also built on the clichés of popular culture and its entertainments, doesn't work as critique because it always remains at the level of parody; it becomes nostalgic, campy.) Though the piece plays with schlock imagery, Breuer's critical intelligence keeps it from becoming kitsch.

The morality of form I think is clear in the spatial poetics delineated in Rose's living quarters, and which is identified in the image track. For example, the bathroom is identified as the place of pride; the kitchen is the scene of hate; the den is the seat of power. Working with the notion of behavior in a particular space Breuer designates special areas for the "sins" lovers commit. While Rose is making creme puffs (one of Breuer's idiosyncratic puns) in her kitchen, the image track, guided by the voices of the speakers, is telling her: DON'T LAUGH ROSE . THE WORD IS . HATE . "Interior decoration" is equated with Rose's state of mind. Functioning in this way, the rooms go beyond being environments and move toward the concept of theological space. If SHAGGY DOG isn't quite a "divine comedy," it is a comedy of manners with a moral persuasion: a parable in the manner of Kafka. Though Breuer probably didn't have topoanalysis (Bachelard's term) in mind, it seems likely his ideas about the behavioral aspects of space were influenced by the artist Gordon Matta-Clark who worked on part of

26 SHAGGY DOG's design. In any case, this sensitivity to behavior and space is a concern one can trace in the work of such artists as Vito Acconci, Bruce Nauman, Robert Smithson, and Mel Bochner to name a few, while at the same time being another example of Breuer's familiarity with current art theory.

Rose's own sojourn into the art world—she does it because she has to support her litter (here again the theme of parental responsibility that runs through the animations)—is humorously chronicled in Part I of the play. Now she satirizes art, patrons, critics, and grantsmanship:

> I LEARNED TO SHAKE HANDS . PLAY DEAD . AND BEG . TWO WEEKS LATER I PICKED UP A CAPS GRANT .

While these lines follow on the sound track, the image track, which relates to it both contrapuntally and analogically, puns on SEE YOURSELF AS A HEAVYWEIGHT as Muhammed Ali's physical measurements are listed. This is typical of the way the humor of the piece grows out of the eccentric wedding of metaphors in the two tracks. And in this case, the way humor plays with the imagery: THE SCENE OF YOUR BOMBER JACKET DRAPED ON A PRESTO LOG . IN A FIELD OF LEFTOVER RAVIOLI . COURTESY RAUSCHENBERG . Much of the fun of SHAGGY DOG rests with the reader's capacity to understand its references which they can only do by being part of a certain society or group. The link is anthropological.

Rose soon tires of the "sub rosa" tactics of the art world and decides to leave it; for her, it's an act of liberation. It is no surprise that Rose is the only one of the animals in the animations who has a name; she is the only one with a clear idea of her selfhood. In an autobiographical sense, the animations move from RED HORSE, which has to do with self-definition, and B.BEAVER, with the acceptance of creative impulses, to SHAGGY DOG, which portrays an artist with a clear idea of self and art. In other words, a shift from self criticism to a criticism of the system that represents a ten year development in the consciousness of a writer. THE SHAGGY DOG ANIMATION brings together all the techniques and themes of the trilogy in a work of stunning lyrical beauty and depth of perception whose authenticity of emotion is quite extraordinary.

■

In the animations Lee Breuer has created a language that only the animations know and whose narrator is known only to them. It is the language of an imagination at once seductive, witty, eccentric, and enormously aware of how writing prompts thinking. The animations reject a bourgeois value system based on the demands of a consumer culture and the dramaturgy it creates to reflect itself. And they reject the notion of a reader consumed by the text in favor of one who can collaborate in its making by allowing another "culture" to grow from it. The result is writing that provides space for the imagination to play in, in the play each reader imagines.

Bonnie Marranca
January-February, 1979
New York City

THE RED HORSE ANIMATION

for **JOANNE AKALAITIS** AND **DAVID WARRILOW**

Mabou Mines premièred a first version of THE RED HORSE
ANIMATION at the Guggenheim Museum, New York, in 1970. The
production was later revised and expanded for a presentation in 1972 at
the Whitney Museum, New York. Written and conceived for the stage by
Lee Breuer. Produced and realized by Mabou Mines.

Cast . . . . JoAnne Akalaitis, Ruth Maleczech,
                                  David Warrilow
Music . . . . Philip Glass
Lighting . . . . Jene Highstein
Wrestling Mat . . . . Tina Girouard
Wall . . . . Power Boothe
Floor . . . . Richard Hayton and Tom Reid

OUTLINE

WHY PRETEND I CAN
DESCRIBE MYSELF . I
SEE MYSELF IN
EVERYTHING THAT
WALKS AND TALKS
AND CRAWLS ON ITS
BELLY . OR JUST LIES
THERE .

WHY NOT PRETEND MY
LIFE HAS COLOR . I
LIKE RED .

WHY NOT PRETEND MY
LIFE HAS FORM . I SEE
AN OUTLINE .

LIFELINE

WHY PRETEND MY
ACTS MEAN ONE THING
RATHER THAN
ANOTHER . WHY
PRETEND IT'S ALL LAID
OUT LIKE THE LINE ON
MY HAND .

STORYLINE

WHY PRETEND TO BE
ORIGINAL . IT'S SO
MUCH WORK .

I FEEL ANOTHER LIFE
LINE . IT'S LIKE
BREATHING SEPARATE
FROM MY OWN .
HOARSE . INANIMATE .
SOMETIMES I THINK IT
TAKES ME OVER . IT'S
BETTER WHEN WE
WORK TOGETHER . THE
BREATH EXPANDS ME .
I ANIMATE THE
BREATH .

I SEE THE FORM .

I ANIMATE THE
BREATH .

NEXT TO A STORYLINE .
OTHER LINES ARE
INCIDENTAL .

I WAS NEVER
WEALTHY . NOT
PARTICULARLY
STRONG . HAD
LEANINGS . ONE DAY I
WAS LEANING EIGHT
DEGREES . THOUGHT I
WAS FALLING ON MY
FACE . BUT NO . IT
WAS EVERYTHING
AROUND ME LEANING
EIGHT DEGREES THE
OTHER WAY . THEN
ALL AT ONCE MY LIFE
WENT FLAT . ALL

I DON'T TRUST IT . IT
COULD PLAY ME FOR A
SUCKER .

I TRUST IT .

I'VE GOT A SHAPE NOT
MINE . I THINK IT'S
THE SHAPE OF THINGS
TO COME . IT'S NOT
CLEAR .

I'M CHANGING .
WHAT AM I .

WHAT AM I .

ALONG THERE'D BEEN
A SLOW LEAK . IN MY
SPACE .

CAN'T MOVE . THAT'S
THE STORY . NEED
SOMEWHERE TO GO .
NEED SOMETHING
STRONG TO CARRY
ME . IT'S AN OLD
STORY . HOW SHALL I
PUT IT .

I'VE GOT IT .

WHERE THE HELL DID I
GET IT .

THE GOBI DESERT .

WHERE DOES IT COME
FROM . I LOOK INTO
EVERYTHING .

I LOOK AT MY FACE .

THE SHAPE . I CAN'T
SEE IT IN MY FACE . I
LOOK AT MY LIFE .

I'VE CHANGED . I'M
NOT MYSELF .

35

DO I OWE A DEBT TO
THE CINEMA .

GENGHIS KHAN
CONQUERS THE WORLD
SUPPLIED BY VISUAL
AIDS TO ELEMENTARY
EDUCATION .

THE BACK ROW . THE
FIRST FORM . RIGHT
INDEX FINGER IN THE
INKWELL . THE LEFT IN
THE HOLE . IN MY
POCKET . WORKING
AWAY . MONGOLS LEAP
THE CARPATHIANS
INTO TRANSYLVANIA
WAS THE SUBTITLE OF
MY FIRST HARD ON .

36 THE SHAPE . I CAN'T
SEE IT IN MY LIFE . I
LOOK FOR MY SPIRIT .

I FEEL MY PULSE . I
FEEL MY SPIRIT . LIKE
A PULSE . ON A
TRACK . LIKE A VEIN .
UNDER WAY . IN A
FINGER . I FEEL MY
RED SPIRIT .

THE GOBI DESERT IS
177,521 SQUARE
MILES . THE GOBI
DESERT IS RED AND
YELLOW . THERE ARE
QUICK CHANGES OF
TEMPERATURE AND
STRONG WINDS . THE
SPACE IS UNCLAIMED
BY THE AVERAGE
URBAN IMAGINATION .
THERE ARE TWO WAYS
TO CROSS THE GOBI
DESERT . ONE'S A
CAMEL .

I TAKE A STEP . I HEAR
TWO FOOTFALLS . I
TAKE TWO STEPS . I
HEAR FOUR FOOTFALLS .
FOUR FOOTED .

I STOP

AND THINK . TWO
FOOTFALLS ARE MINE .
AND TWO ARE ECHO .

THERE'S SOMETHING
WRONG ABOUT A
CAMEL .

SHOULD KNOW BETTER
THAN TO THINK .

QUESTION OF STYLE .
MY STYLE . A CAMEL'S
STYLE .

THINKING LEAVES ME
WITH MY ECHO .

I LOOK AT MY SPIRIT .

I LOOK AT MY SPIRIT . I
SEE A MAP OF ALL THE
PATHS . AND ALL THE
PLACES THEY'RE
SUPPOSED TO GO . I
SEE WHERE I'M AT .
IT'S WHERE I'VE
ALWAYS BEEN . I'M
NOT WELL TRAVELED .

SO I STUDY THE MAP .
I SEE WHERE I WANT TO
GO . WHERE THINGS
ARE AT . I TAKE A
PENCIL . A BLUE
PENCIL AND I NUMBER
EACH THING . THEN I
STEP BACK AND LOOK
AT ALL MY NUMBERS .

THEN I DRAW A LINE
FROM ONE NUMBER TO
ANOTHER WITH THE
BLUE PENCIL .

THEN I LOOK AT WHAT
I'VE DRAWN .

A BLUE KNOT .

SO I CHANGE PENCILS .
I TAKE A RED PENCIL

38 AND I DRAW A LINE
BETWEEN THE
NUMBERS .

NOTHING'S THERE . NO
NUMBERS . I MAKE UP
MY OWN .

I LOOK AT WHAT I'VE
DRAWN WITH A RED
PENCIL .

IT FEELS COLD .

THERE'S SOMETHING
COLD BETWEEN MY
TEETH . IT INSTRUCTS
ME . IT TURNS ME
WHERE IT WANTS ME
TO GO .

A RED HORSE .

ELEVEN SEVEN .

IN THE DAYS OF
GENGHIS KHAN .

A ROMANCE .

■ THE RED HORSE .
■ THE ANIMATION OF AN OUTLINE .
■ ROMAN NUMERAL ONE .
  IN WHICH I DEMONSTRATE MY
  SOUND .

  THINK I SEE AN OUTLINE .
■ ROMAN NUMERAL TWO .
■ IN WHICH I THINK I SEE MY
  SHAPE .

TIC A TAH **DAH** . TIC A TAH **DAH** . TIC A TAH **DAH DAH** . TIC A TAH
DAH . TIC A TAH **DAH DAH** . TIC A TAH **DAH DAH DAH** . TIC A TAH
DAH . TIC A TAH **DAH DAH** . TIC A TAH **DAH DAH DAH** . TIC A TAH
DAH DAH DAH DAH . TIC A TAH **DAH** . TIC A TAH **DAH DAH** . TIC A
TAH **DAH** . TIC A TAH **DAH DAH** . TIC A TAH **DAH DAH DAH** . TIC A
TAH **DAH DAH DAH DAH**. TIC A TAH **DAH** . TIC A TAH **DAH DAH** . TIC
A TAH **DAH DAH DAH** . TIC A TAH **DAH** . TIC A TAH **DAH DAH** . TIC A
TAH **DAH DAH DAH** . TIC A TAH **DAH DAH DAH DAH** . TIC A TAH
DAH . TIC A TAH **DAH** . TIC A TAH **DAH DAH** . TIC A TAH **DAH DAH**
DAH . TIC A TAH **DAH** . TIC A TAH **DAH DAH** .TIC A TAH **DAH DAH**
DAH . TIC A TAH **DAH DAH DAH DAH** . TIC A TAH **DAH** . TIC A TAH
DAH DAH . TIC A TAH **DAH** . TIC A TAH **DAH DAH** . TIC A TAH **DAH**
DAH DAH . TIC A TAH **DAH** . TIC A TAH **DAH DAH** . TIC A TAH **DAH**
DAH DAH . TIC A TAH **DAH DAH DAH DAH** . TIC A TAH **DAH** . TIC A
TAH **DAH** . TIC A TAH **DAH DAH** . TIC A TAH **DAH** . TIC A TAH **DAH**
DAH . TIC A TAH **DAH DAH DAH** . TIC A TAH **DAH** . TIC A TAH **DAH**
DAH . TIC A TAH **DAH DAH DAH** . TIC A TAH **DAH DAH DAH DAH** .

THAT'S MY SOUND NOW .

I DON'T THINK I USED TO SOUND LIKE MUCH OF ANYTHING . I THINK
I'M MAKING THINGS UP AS I GO ALONG . I'VE COME ALONG . I'M IN A
DIFFERENT PLACE . I GUESS THAT MEANS THIS ISN'T THE BEGINNING .

IF THIS WERE THE END AND I WERE STILL HERE MAKING THINGS UP .
I'D BE CRAZY . I DON'T THINK I'M CRAZY . SO I THINK THIS IS THE
MIDDLE .

CONFUSION IN THE MIDDLE . WHAT NOW . WHAT AM I . CAN'T TELL
MUCH . I THINK I'M TRAVELING . I GUESS IT'S NIGHT . CAN'T SEE THE
TAIL ON MY BUTT . CAN'T SEE THE NOSE ON MY MUZZLE . THINK I SEE
SOMETHING ELSE .

AN OUTLINE . MOVING IN THE TREES . MAKING TRACKS . THE MOON
ATTACHED TO MY LEFT SHOULDER BY A STRAP . HOW I PULL IT OVER
MOUNTAINS . THROUGH LAKES . MY COLOR . I CAN JUST MAKE IT OUT
BY MOONLIGHT . RED .

I GO THROUGH MY CHANGES . FORWARDS . AND BACKWARDS .
SOONER . OR LATER . I'LL COME TO WHERE I AM . I THINK . I'LL COME
TO MYSELF . I MUST HAVE STARTED SOMEWHERE . AND WORKED MY
WAY HERE . TO THE MIDDLE . HOW DID I DO IT . CAN'T SEE HOW .
CAN'T SEE THAT . IN THE OUTLINE . THE RED HORSE . CAN'T KEEP IT
GOING .

■ CAPITAL LETTER A .
DO I OWE A DEBT TO THE CINEMA .

ELEVEN SEVEN . GENGHIS KHAN INSTITUTES THE CRAFT OF DELIVERY .
BY HORSE . CUT . PAN OF THE GOBI DESERT . CUT . A JUJUBE TREE .
CUT . A RED HORSE . ZOOM . WITH RIDER . TRACK . IN THE DAYS OF
GENGHIS KHAN RED HORSES WERE RESERVED FOR SPECIAL JOURNEYS .
THEY CARRIED MESSAGES . WRAPPED AROUND ARROWS . TO INDICATE
POST HASTE . THEY SPENT THEIR LIVES CROSSING THE GOBI DESERT .
WHIPPED CRAZY . STATION TO STATION . THEN HOBBLED . SAY .
MONTHS . WAITING . WHILE THE MESSAGE THEY CARRIED WAS
RELAYED ON .

EACH LIFE . SAY EACH CROSSING . ONE HORSE CARRIED FOUR
HUNDRED DIFFERENT MESSAGES . EACH . ONE FOUR HUNDREDTH OF
THE WAY . CARRIED . SAY . **VICTORY IS OURS** . OVER THE CHO-RIN-GEE
ROCK BASIN . THEN . **ALL IS LOST** . THE RED HORSE CARRIES . ALL IS
LOST . IN SNOW . IN CIRCLES . SAY . IN THE MIDDLE OF ITS PASSAGE
WOULD NOT SAID HORSE BECOME CONFUSED . ABOUT THE TRUTH OF
WHAT IT WAS CONVEYING . WOULD IT NOT CRAVE A CONSTANT PIECE
OF INFORMATION TO DELIVER . SAY . FOR DELIVERANCE . COULD NOT
IT THEN PERCEIVE ITS GOING . AS ITS BEING . IN THE DESERT . SAY .
GOBI DESERT . COULD IT NOT DELIVER . THEN . ITS MOTION . WRAPPED
AROUND AN ARROW . SAY . ITS DANCE .

LET US GO BACK AND TELL THE STORY OF ONE SUCH HORSE . GO BACK .
AND TELL THE STORY OF . GO BACK . RIDER . CUT . HORSE . GO BACK .
JUJUBE TREE . GO BACK . GOBI DESERT . GENGHIS KHAN . ELEVEN
SEVEN .

■ AND B .
I GET MOVING AGAIN .

AND STAY ON THE TRACK . I ENTER A GORGE . THE PATH RUNS ALONG
A STREAM . I CAN SEE MYSELF . IN THE STREAM . MOVING ALONG
WITH ME . SAY . IT IS MY IMAGINATION . SAY IT . MY REFLECTION IS
MY IMAGINATION .

HOW I TURN IT BACK . BEHIND ME .
BY TURNING TOWARD THE MOON .

HOW I USE MY IMAGINATION .

■ ARABIC NUMERAL ONE .
HOW I GET A LITTLE DRAMA INTO
MY LIFE .

I REMEMBER NOTHING . WHERE I CAME FROM . HOW I GOT HERE .
NOTHING .

OUR FIELD . GOOD . THE FENCE . THE WATER . HOW I MAKE IT ALL UP
FROM THE BEGINNING . MY BIRTH . MY OLD SIRE . THE NIGHT . HOW I
HOLD ME IN MY ARMS AND TELL ME A STORY .

THE MANNER IN WHICH I TROTTED BY MY SIRE'S SIDE . IN A CIRCLE .
INSIDE HIS CIRCLE . ON THE THRESHING FLOOR . LEARNING ABOUT
BREAD . MY SIRE'S NAME WAS DAILY BREAD .

FIELD . FENCE . AND SO ON . MY BIRTH . FIRST SAW THE LIGHT . AT
NIGHT . WEANED FROM TIT . TO GRASS . MY DAM . ONE OF THE HERD .
YEAH . MEMORIES OF CHILDHOOD . YEAH . HAD IT FAT . PLAYED
GAMES . PLAYED STUPID . THE BULL THAT USED TO JUMP THE FENCE
INTO OUR FIELD TO DROP HIS LOAD . MY SIRE . HE ALWAYS ADVISED
ME TO LEAVE WELL ENOUGH ALONE . BECAUSE IT MADE THE GRASS
GROW . MY SIRE LIKED TO FEEL THE GRASS GROW . UNDER HIS FEET .
MY SIRE'S NAME WAS DAILY BREAD .

■ TWO .
IN WHICH I GET INVOLVED .

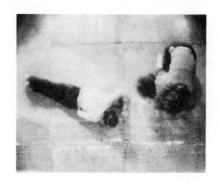 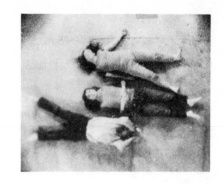

HOW I MAKE BELIEVE I'M NOT ALONE . THAT MY SIRE'S WITH ME .
ALWAYS . I BELIEVE IT . I CAN CONTACT HIM .

GOOD EVENING SIRE . CAN YOU HEAR ME . **YES** . CAN YOU SEE ME . **NO** .

I FORGOT ABOUT THE BLINDERS . HE WORE BLINDERS .

OH YEAH . WORKING BACK .

MOVING ON . THINGS GO BY . I MUST BE MAKING HEADWAY . WHERE
WAS I .

OH YEAH . GETTING INVOLVED .

DAILY BREAD COULD ALWAYS HEAR ME . I WAS NEVER IN STEP WITH
HIM . BUT DAILY BREAD COULD NEVER SEE ME . OFF TO THE SIDE . HE
WORE BLINDERS .

HE COULDN'T SEE ME UNLESS I STOOD IN FRONT OF HIM . WHICH WAS
IMPOSSIBLE . HE NEVER STOPPED . HE WOULD HAVE RUN ME OVER .
HE COULDN'T SEE ME UNLESS I WERE TO BACK UP . IN HIS LINE OF
VISION . RIGHT AROUND THE THRESHING FLOOR .

I THOUGHT OF DOING IT . BUT IT WOULD HAVE BEEN INSULTING . AS MUCH AS DAILY BREAD WAS INTO BREAD . HE WAS MORE INTO CIRCLES .

HE WAS ONE FOR TRADITION . TRADITIONALLY . ONE SHUTS UP TILL ONE CAN SAY A MOUTHFUL . THEN ONE SPEAKS ONE'S PIECE . IT'S QUITE AN OCCASION . TRADITIONALLY . AFTER A LIFE OF RETICENCE . ONE PASSES ON . WHAT ONE'S SEEN . WHERE ONE'S BEEN . A WORD OR TWO ABOUT THE WAY ONE'S TAKEN . TO THE OTHERS . ALL THE OTHERS IN THE FIELD . THEN . TRADITIONALLY . ONE'S OVER . PLOP . UNDERGROUND .

AND SO IN THE GOOD HARVEST OF HIS YEARS MY OLD SIRE PREPARES TO SPEAK . HE PRACTICES EACH DAY DURING HIS ROUNDS . I HEAR HIM . STOP . IN HIS TRACKS . ON HIS CIRCLE . ON THE THRESHING FLOOR . TO PAW THE CHAFF . TO PONDER . THE SALUTATION .

MY FOALS . **NO** . MY FRUITS . **NO** . MY FOLIAGE . **AHEM** . UNACCUSTOMED AS I AM . **NO** . I LIMIT MYSELF . TO JUST A FEW . TO JUST A WORD . TO THE WISE .

AND THEN THE CRACK . AS I RECALL . HE STOPS REHEARSING AT THE CRACK . AND CAN'T GO ON . **CRACK** .

AND THAT'S AS FAR AS HE CAN GET . BEFORE HE GETS HIS ASS WHIPPED . GUESS A BEAST . CAN'T SPEAK HIS PIECE . AND BEAR HIS BURDEN .

THE THRESHERS DON'T CARE WHAT THE FUCK YOU SAY . SIRE . OR HOW YOU PREPARE IT . SO LONG AS YOU DON'T STOP TO DO IT . DON'T YOU GET IT . EVERYTIME YOU STOP TO THINK . SOMEBODY LOSES DAILY BREAD .

CAN'T YOU SPEAK IN THE FIELD AT NIGHT . ARE THE SMELLS OF THE FLOWERS DISTRACTING . WE'RE FOREVER LISTENING . WE SLEEP WITH OUR EARS COCKED . AND OUR EYES OPEN . CAN'T YOU SEE US . ALL . MOONS IN THE GRASS .

NOT A SOUND .

MY SIRE WAS NOT INTO THE NIGHT . WHAT COULD HE SAY . HE WAS INTO CIRCLES .

CONCLUSION . THE HOT SEASON .

HOW ALL THE WORLD WAS BREATHING BADLY . NOT A DOG COULD BARK WITHOUT COUGHING FIRST . THE WAY WE LIVED . SNEEZING FLIES . AND KNEE DEEP IN A LOAD OF BULL AND —

CONCLUSION . HOW I CONCLUDE .

THAT DAILY BREAD WAS OF THAT SPECIAL BREED . A HORSE'S ASS .

ITEM . HIS DILEMMA.

THAT HE COULD NOT SPEAK WHILE MOVING . THAT HE COULD NOT MOVE WHILE SPEAKING . AND SO EVERYTIME HE STOPPED TO START .

ITEM . HE GOT HIS ASS WHIPPED .

ITEM . HIS BRIGHT IDEA .

HE WOULD WORK A NIGHT SHIFT IN THE THRESHER ALL ALONE .

ITEM . HIS PRACTICALITY .

NOT ONLY COULD HE SPEAK HIS PIECE . HE'D MAKE MORE BREAD .

ITEM . HOW MY OLD SIRE PROCEEDED FORTHWITH TO THE THRESHER .

ITEM . THE ZEAL THAT HE DISPLAYED .

ITEM . THAT HE GALLOPED .

ITEM . THAT HE LEAPED THE FENCE AROUND OUR FIELD .

THE CRACK .

HOW HE SPOKE . THEN .

WHO HE WAS SPEAKING TO .

THAT IT WAS A LEAP OF THE IMAGINATION . THAT HE IMAGINED . DAILY BREAD . WHAT COULD YOU HAVE IMAGINED . THE ROPE AROUND HIS NECK TIED TO A STAKE STUCK IN THE GROUND . ITS LENGTH . THE LENGTH OF HIS LEAPING .

HOW IN MIDAIR IT CRACKED HIS WINDPIPE .

FREELY .

ME .

THERE WERE NO OTHERS IN THE FIELD .

HOW I COULDN'T UNDERSTAND A WORD HE WAS SAYING . WITH HIS WINDPIPE CRACKED HE COULDN'T MAKE A SOUND .

THE WAY HE CONCLUDED .

AND WAITED . ON ONE KNEE . DAILY BREAD . WHAT COULD YOU HAVE BEEN WAITING FOR . APPLAUSE I'LL BET . HE WAS FULL OF THAT HORSE SHIT .

A YELLOW STAR APPEARED . TIP OF HIS TONGUE . WHERE THE WISE WORDS WERE . THAT SHOULD HAVE BEEN MINE . TRADITIONALLY .

FADE .

I LOOK DOWN . I CAN SEE MY
STORY .

■ ROMAN NUMERAL THREE .
I COME TO WHERE I AM .

■ THE RED HORSE .
■ THE ANIMATION OF AN OUTLINE .
■ ROMAN NUMERAL ONE .

■ ROMAN NUMERAL FOUR .
IN WHICH I .

■ ROMAN NUMERAL FIVE .

THEY WERE STILL IN HIS MOUTH . I COULD TELL HIS TONGUE WAS
GOLDEN . I . BIT . IT . . OUT . . . AND . HAVING . LEARNED . .
NOTHING . . ABOUT . . . CIRCLES . . . I . . STARTED . . .
RUNNING . . . .

LIKE A REFLECTION . PULLING EVEN WITH ME ON THE SURFACE OF THE
STREAM . I CAN FEEL MY LIFE AND MY IMAGINATION COMING
TOGETHER .

AND HAVING LEARNED NOTHING ABOUT CIRCLES I STARTED RUNNING
IN A LINE .

NO .

NO . IN WHICH I . YES . SOMEWHERE . NO . IN THE MIDDLE . YES . COME
TO KNOW . YES . WHERE I AM . NO . COME TO KNOW . YES . SOME OF
MY NEEDS .

ONE . SOME FORM TO HOLD ME .

TWO . SOME FORCE TO CHANGE ME .

THREE . SOME MOTION TO CARRY ME .

FOUR . SOME WAY TO GO .

FIVE . SOME FORM TO HOLD ME .

FIVE . SOME FORM TO HOLD ME .

ONE . SOME FORM TO HOLD ME . THE RED HORSE . YES . THE RED
HORSE .

50

VOICES

```
              C        C  C          C  CC
A  A  A                AAAA         AAAAAAA
G  GGG  G             GGGG          GGGGGGG
 E   EE                 EE           EE   EE
```

```
C  CC  C             C  CC            C  C
AAAAAAAAA           AAAAAAA          AAAA
GGGGGGGGG           GGGGGGG          GGGG
 EE   EE  E           EE   EE          EE
```

VOICES AND HOOVES

```
C  C                 C  CC            C  CC  C
AAAA                AAAAAAA          AAAAAAAAA
GGGG                GGGGGGG          GGGGGGGGG
 EE                   EE   EE          EE   EE  E
 I..I..                I..I..  I..I      I..I..  I..I  I..
```

```
C  CC                C  C
AAAAAAA             AAAA
GGGGGGG             GGGG
 EE   EE              EE
 I..I..  I..I          I..I..
```

HOOVES

```
I..I..           I..I....  I..I..    I..I....  I..I..
I..I  I..I        I..I..  I..I  I..   I..I  I..
```

DON'T KNOW WHAT TO CALL
IT . DON'T KNOW WHAT TO
CALL .
■ ROMAN NUMERAL SIX .

AS OPPOSED TO MOVING IT'S AT A STANDSTILL . IT'S LIKE A FEVER AS
OPPOSED TO A CHILL . THERE ARE VOICES THAT I HEAR WHEN I'M NOT
SPEAKING . I SEE THINGS . I'M NOT MYSELF .

HOW IN MY ILLNESS I SEE
SOMETHING .

MY LIFE SOMEWHERE . AND HOW IT COMES TO ME THAT I AM A
REPRESENTATION . THE WAY I SUSPECT THAT I'M NOT WELL
REPRESENTED . THAT I'M NOT WELL .

■ ROMAN NUMERAL SEVEN .
SHOWING THE ILLNESS .

HOW THE RED HORSE .

TEARS ITSELF APART . AND TRIES TO HOLD ITSELF TOGETHER .

YOU'VE BEEN HERE BEFORE . HERE'S WHERE YOU STOP . THIS IS THE
PLACE .

THAT'S RIGHT . THAT'S ALL .

M O V E

LOSS . OF CONNECTION .

HERE'S WHERE YOU CUT OFF . NO MISTAKE . LOOK AT THE TIME . YOU
STOP TRUSTING . YOU CAN'T FEEL A THING .

NOW YOU JUST GO THROUGH
YOUR MOTIONS .
■ NUMBER SEVEN .
DO YOUR SHOW .

WIPE YOURSELF OUT . OUT OF THE GORGE . GO ON . INTO THE LIGHT .
YOU CAN SEE YOUR WAY . YOUR DUST . YOUR METHODS .

YOU CAN SEE THROUGH YOURSELF .

LOSS . OF CREDIBILITY .

NAME . THE RED HORSE . **BORN** . ELEVEN SEVEN . **NOW RESIDING** . IN THE
MIDDLE . **COLOR** . SEE ABOVE . **BRIEF DESCRIPTION** . A ROMANCE . **NAME** . THE
RED HORSE—

LOSS . OF
IMAGINATION .

I CAN'T HELP YOU . I CAN'T FIND YOU .

ITEM . LOSS . OF
MIND .

YOU . LOSE . IT .

  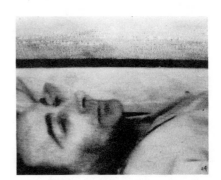

THE B.BEAVER ANIMATION

for **FREDERICK NEUMANN**

Mabou Mines premièred THE B.BEAVER ANIMATION jointly at the
Museum of Modern Art, New York, as part of the program "A Valentine for
Marcel Duchamp," and at the Theater for the New City, New York, in
1974. Written and conceived for the stage by Lee Breuer. Produced and
realized by Mabou Mines.

Cast	JoAnne Akalaitis, Ruth Maleczech, Frederick Neumann, Bill Raymond, David Warrilow (Bill Raymond's part was originally performed by Dawn Gray)
Dam	Tina Girouard (Adapted for performance by Steven Benneyworth, Thom Cathcart, and Terry O'Reilly)
Light Frames	Thom Cathcart
Curtain Puppetry	Terry O'Reilly
Light Ball	Stephen Bennyworth

EXCUSE ME . WHEN I'M ADDRESSED I'M EMBARRASSED . I ASSUME
YOU'RE THE SAME . MORE PRECISELY I'M SELF EFFACED .
ACCORDINGLY ALLOW ME TO PRESENT TO YOU THE B.BEAVER . WHILE I
FLEE . YOU CAN PRESENT TO ME ANYTHING YOU WANT . THAT'S YOUR
STORY .

TO DO ME JUSTICE I'VE BEEN KNOWN TO TURN AROUND AND RAGE
WHILE WALKING BACKWARDS . I RAGE AT ELEMENTS . SPRING . AND
FISH . TUNA FISH . TAKE TUNA FISH . ONCE A YEAR THEY COME OUT
OF THE SEA TO WREAK THEIR HAVOC ON HONEST LABOR . GRANTED
THEY'RE COLD BLOODED . THEY KNOW NOT WHAT THEY DO . I CONCEDE
THERE ARE MORAL ANOMALIES IN THE HARD CORE ANTITUNIAST .
BUT . WHEN YOU SEE THEM SWARMING IN THE CURRENT . WATCH
THEM RIFLE RAPIDS . CLIMB CATARACTS AND DAMS . TAKE BEAVER
DAMS . THE WORLD'S FINEST BLEND OF CHOICE SILTS ORGANIC
COMPOST EARTHY ALKALIS FRESH BROOK SHALE NOT TO MENTION
LABOR . RESEARCH . CREATIVE LEADERSHIP . GO IN TO DAMMING . THE
FLOW . I'VE SEEN A TUNA FISH LOWER ITS HEAD AND GO RIGHT
THROUGH A STURDY LITTLE FABRICATION LIKE A BULLET .

I PERSIST IN THIS FICTION . I'VE ACHIEVED A DAILY FICTION . PRIOR TO
THIS ACHIEVEMENT IT WAS DAILY BLOTTO . THE MISSUS USED TO
THROW MY EMPTY BOTTLES INTO THE POOL . ALL NIGHT THEY'D
NUZZLE . EXCUSE ME BUT YOU CAUGHT THAT DIDN'T YOU . SALMON .
CALLING SALMON TUNA FISH . I HAVE ENEMIES . I CAN'T PRONOUNCE
THEIR NAMES . THEY ESCAPE . UNCANNY LITTLE FUCKERS .

DAILY FICTION . SPRING . GATHERING THE BROOD . WE SIT ATOP THE
DAM AND WATCH THE SNOW ATOP THE MOUNTAIN . BEHOLD SNOW . I
SAY . IT'S WHITE . TO BE EXACT . AND . COLD TO BE SPECIFIC . A
FORCE OF NATURE . IN THE SUN IT FLASHES LIKE A BRIGHT IDEA .

B.BEAVER IS A STUTTERER .
HE'S A SMALL COMMUTER
TRAIN OF SPLIT PERSONALITIES
ALL READING FOR HIS PART .
OUT OF SYNC .

B.BEAVER MOVES ME WHEN
HE IS MOST INNATELY A RAT .

60 THAT IS . WHEN THE SUN SHINES YOU GET FLASHES .
EXCUSE ME BUT I BECOME THE PEDAGOGUE IN DEALING WITH
PHENOMENA . PERORATIONS ON GEOLOGICAL FORMATIONS .
HYDRAULICS . THAWS . HOW SNOW THAWS . PERFORCE FALLING DOWN
MOUNTAINS . PERFORCE LIFTING STREAMS . THE BROOD . THEY
SHIVER . THEY DRIP . THEY WIPE THEIR NOSES ON THEIR TAILS . I
PLUNGE AHEAD INTO THE EQUILIBRIUM OF NATURE .

NO I DON'T .

MY CORRESPONDENCE . KEEP UP WITH MY CORRESPONDENCE . I KNOCK
OFF THE FIRST LINE IN LATIN . EPISTOLUM RODANTUM AMPHIBIUM AD LIBRARIUM
LOCALUM .

LATIN . THIS IS A SECRET
NOTE TO MYSELF THAT PART
OF THE BEAVER LIVES ON
AVENUE B BETWEEN 5TH AND
6TH STREETS OVER THE
MUCHO MACHO SOCIAL CLUB .

AS YOU KNOW IN RECENT YEARS OUR WINTERS HAVE BEEN LIGHT . YET
MAY I POINT OUT THAT DUE TO CURIOUS CONSIDERATIONS .
METEOROLOGICAL CONFIGURATIONS . CUMULO NIMBUS . UPDRAFT .
PRECIPITATE OZONE . AND A STATIONARY FRONT . I HAVE OBSERVED
FROM ATOP MY DAM CONSIDERABLE SNOW ON THE MOUNTAIN .

NOW LET US SAY v IS THE VOLUME OF SNOW . LET US CONJECTURE .
THE SNOW IS x MANY INCHES . ONE ALLOWS FOR i AN INCREASE
TOWARD THE TOP . ONE TAKES THE m MEAN OF THE i INCREASE FROM
THE TIMBERLINE TL TO s SUMMIT . IT'S SIMPLE ALGEBRA .

CONSIDER THERE ARE TT TRIBUTARY TRICKLES . TRICKLES . MIND YOU .
I UNDERLINE . TRICKLES . THAT p PLUMMET DOWN THROUGH THE TREES .
OVER PRECIPICES . UNDER r ROCKS c CATARACTING OVER CLIFFS .
THROUGH VALLEYS . THESE FORM f FIVE g GENTLE BROOKS . ONE OF
THESE BROOKS IS MB MY BROOK . ONE FIFTH OF THAT SNOW IS MS MY

SNOW . WERE IT ALL TO THAW AND HURTLE DOWN . MY BROOK WOULD
COME TO BE т TORRENT s SWEEPING EVERYTHING BEFORE IT . IT
WOULD SWEEP MY ᴅᴀᴍ DAM BEFORE IT . TO ʀ RIVERS . TO s SEA ᴄ
CARAMBA . THAT'S A ᴅᴇʟᴜɢᴇ FLOOD .

HEART THUMPING . TAIL THUMPING . GOOD GOD A TRAUMA . I
CRUMPLE UP THE LETTER AND THROW IT OUT THE WINDOW . THEN I
THROW ME OUT THE WINDOW . LOOK AT THAT . PANIC . SLAVE OF THE
SUBCONSCIOUS .

PERISH . THE THOUGHT .

SUMMONING SANG FROID I CRAWL BACK TO MY DESK . SUCK IN MY
LINEA SEMILUNARIS . AND SELECT A POSTCARD . WILDLIFE
COMPOSITION .

WOULD YOU BE SO KIND AS TO SEND ME WHAT YOU HAVE ON
FRESHWATER DAMNATION . SOMETHING IN THE DO IT YOURSELF SERIES
WOULD BE MOST HELPFUL . MATERIAL ESTIMATES . ANYTHING
TECHNICAL ON STRESSES . BLUEPRINTS . NOT TO NEGLECT PURE
THEORY . MARGINALIA . ESOTERICA . THE RELATED SCIENCES .
CLAUSEWITZ ON BARRICADES . IN SHORT . THE WORKS . ON THE
SUBJECT .

I ADD A POSTSCRIPT . I WRITE SMALL . PRESUMING YOU FIND IT
STRANGE . ONE OF MY ILK WITHOUT THIS INFORMATION AT HIS
FINGERTIPS . BORN BUILDER AND SUCH . WELL . I HAD IT .
MISPLACED . MISHANDLED . SWIPED . YOU KNOW THE MISSUS MAY
HAVE THROWN IT INTO THE TRASH . DON'T GET ME STARTED ON THE
MISSUS . IT'S LOST . THAT'S A FACT . I AM A BEAVER WHO HAS LOST
THE ART OF DAMNATION AT A CRUCIAL TIME . AND COME HELL OR HIGH
WATER—

B.BEAVER IS ALSO A TURD .
THIS IS A LITERARY
ALLUSION .

AHA! . THE THOUGHT .
PERISH . HERE THE B.BEAVER
DROPS ITS LOAD . OF TWO BY
FOURS . IN THIS CASE . THE
DAM COLLAPSES . CURTAINS
FLAIL . YIKES . EXPLODES
ACROSS THE FRAME . THE
PIECE . THE ANIMATION .
CONSIDERS IT'S DEMISE .

ADDRESS CLEARLY PLEASE . SPARE NO EXPENSE . I EAGERLY AWAIT .

MORNING . THERE WAS NO IMMEDIATE REPLY . EVENING . NEXT MORNING . NEXT EVENING . MORNING . AFTER THAT . THE FOLLOWING EVENING . SCROBIS ID . SCREW IT .

SILENCE OF THE MAILS . COMING OF THE SPRING . ESTRANGEMENT OF THE SOUL . VACATION WEATHER . AFTERNOON . I FLOAT DOWNSTREAM ON MY BACK . SPOUTING WATER .

ALL ALONG THE BROOK BANK THE HUM OF INDUSTRY . PART OF THE GRAND SCHEME . SPRING WORKS . WHEN THE JUICES FLOW . LOOK AT THEM . MYRIAD CREATURES . NOLENS VOLENS . WILLY NILLY . EAT . CRAP . SCREW . CROAK . WHAT STYLE . NO ELABORATION . ID EST UBI EST . THAT'S WHERE IT'S AT .

I GO ASHORE . SPRING WITH A VENGEANCE . GRASS AND FLOWERS . NOTHING STOPS IT . ON THE BANK I STAND UPON A CARPET OF FLOWERS . I WIPE MY FEET .

SADNESS . NO MISTAKE . THAT MAKES ME FURIOUS . LONGING . NO MISTAKE . I CAN FEEL IT GIVING . MY DEAR BARRIER . TO HAVE DEDICATED THE WORK OF MY MATURER YEARS TO DAMMING ALL THAT CRAP UP TO PERFECTION . PAIN . GOD DAMN IT NOW I'M IN PAIN . I CAN'T ACCEPT IT .

PAIN IN ANY OTHER GUISE I'M SURE I COULD ACCEPT . A LION . I'M SURE I COULD ACCEPT A WOUNDED LION . IF ONLY I WERE SOME DUMB ANIMAL . I'D GET A RUNNING START AND SCRAMBLE UP A TREE . WRAP MY TAIL AROUND A BRANCH . AND HANG . I'D PLAY POSSUM .

ESCAPE . AND DREAM . OF MAKING THE WORLD SAFE FOR BEAVERS . CELINE'S SHIP FOUNDERING OVER THE HOTEL DE VILLE . B.BEAVER PUTS UP A SAIL . HIS ROBE . AND THE WIND TURNS IT INTO A GHOST WALKING ON THE WATER . VOICE BY M. MAGOO .

 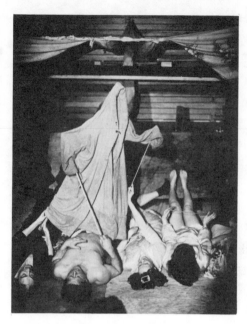 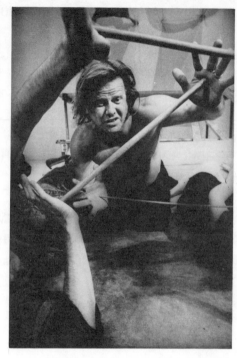

NIGHTS FALL . MOONS RISE . THE YELLOW STARS PUSH THROUGH THE SKY . THE FLOWERS THROUGH THE EARTH . I CAN'T TELL THE DIFFERENCE . HANGING THERE WITH THE PISS SCARED OUT OF ME I CAN'T TELL WHAT'S UP . THAT'S THE FAILURE OF A POINT OF VIEW . I'LL HAVE TO REASSESS . GET ON TOP OF WHAT'S UP . GET RIGHT TO THE BOTTOM OF WHAT'S GOING DOWN . CHRIST SAKE . I'D FLIP . I'D GO UNDER .

PHLOOEY . NOT BAD . NOT BAD AS A HABITAT FOR A COLD FISH . FLORIUS AQUAMARINUS . UNENDING SOURCE OF STIMULATION FOR THE BOTANICALLY INCLINED . PEAS . FROZEN PEAS . EVERYTHING AMAZED DOWN HERE . WIDE EYED AMAZEMENT . AND I'M PARTICULARLY TAKEN WITH THE RETICENCE . FEW BUBBLY GLUBS . NO PRETENSIONS .

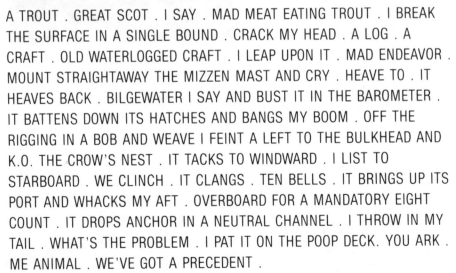

A TROUT . GREAT SCOT . I SAY . MAD MEAT EATING TROUT . I BREAK
THE SURFACE IN A SINGLE BOUND . CRACK MY HEAD . A LOG . A
CRAFT . OLD WATERLOGGED CRAFT . I LEAP UPON IT . MAD ENDEAVOR .
MOUNT STRAIGHTAWAY THE MIZZEN MAST AND CRY . HEAVE TO . IT
HEAVES BACK . BILGEWATER I SAY AND BUST IT IN THE BAROMETER .
IT BATTENS DOWN ITS HATCHES AND BANGS MY BOOM . OFF THE
RIGGING IN A BOB AND WEAVE I FEINT A LEFT TO THE BULKHEAD AND
K.O. THE CROW'S NEST . IT TACKS TO WINDWARD . I LIST TO
STARBOARD . WE CLINCH . IT CLANGS . TEN BELLS . IT BRINGS UP ITS
PORT AND WHACKS MY AFT . OVERBOARD FOR A MANDATORY EIGHT
COUNT . IT DROPS ANCHOR IN A NEUTRAL CHANNEL . I THROW IN MY
TAIL . WHAT'S THE PROBLEM . I PAT IT ON THE POOP DECK. YOU ARK .
ME ANIMAL . WE'VE GOT A PRECEDENT .

WE HIT AN ICEBERG . WE GO DOWN OFF THE COAST OF
NEWFOUNDLAND . DISASTER . I SWIM HOME . THE MOUSE THE MARMOT

66 ALL THE OTHER FURRY LITTLE CREATURES FLOATING FACE DOWN OVER THE INUNDATED EARTH . LITTLE DEAD BALLS . ONLY THE BEAVER PLUNGED ON . STROKE TWO . BREATHE FOUR . ONLY THE BEAVER ESCAPED ALONE TO TELL .
PLUNGING ON . STROKE TWO . BREATHE FOUR . ONLY THE BEAVER ESCAPED ALONE TO TELL .

WAKE UP WITH JOY IN MY HEART . I COME ALIVE NO MATTER WHAT I DO . IT'S KILLING ME . RIGHT . WRITE . WILL AND TESTAMENT . WRITE . BEING OF SOUND . STOP . INCIDENTALLY MY PET . WE'RE RUINED . CLEANED OUT . IF YOU DON'T BELIEVE ME LOOK AT MY TESTAMENT . I'VE NOTHING TO LEAVE . MUCH TO MY REGRET . MY PET . I SUSPECT EMBEZZLEMENT .

ANY IDEAS .

YOU HAVEN'T THE FAINTEST OF IDEAS . I CONFRONTED THE BROOD . NONE OF YOU HAS EVER HAD THE FAINTEST OF IDEAS . YOU DON'T EVEN KNOW HOW THE FAINTEST OF IDEAS IS GONE ABOUT BEING HAD .

ONE FEELS FOXY . THE FAINTEST OF IDEAS MAKES ME FEEL FOXY . I GROW HARD . AND BUSHY TAILED . I LOOK AT MYSELF FULL LENGTH . SMEGMATIC . ERECT . A BLUSH STARTS IN MY TOES AND RISES LIKE A RASPBERRY PHOSPHATE IN A STRAW . I'VE GOT IT .

REINFORCED CONCRETE .

TO THE DRAFTING BOARD . EXCUSE ME MY PET . MY CALLING . IT'S CALLING . I BREAK OUT MY TRIANGLES LAY ON A T SQUARE AND TOP IT OFF WITH TWO DRAFTING PINS AND A FRENCH CURVE . I TAKE A BITE . IT'S DELICIOUS . I DIP IN THE COOLER AND WHIP OUT A COLT FORTY FIVE . REINFORCED CONCRETE CAPTURES THE ANIMAL IMAGINATION . VITAL TO DEFENSE . RESEARCH SUBSIDIZED . LOCAL BEAVER MAKES KILLING IN BROOKSHORE REAL ESTATE . I KNOW WHAT I'M DOING .

READ THAT ANY GIVEN SPECIES REDUCED BY MORE THAN HALF . REDUCED TO PEERING INTO EXTINCTION . STARTS TO MUTATE . SAY EACH MUTATION IS A NEW IDEA ABOUT COMING TO GRIPS . MOST OF THEM ARE RATHER REDUNDANT LIKE TWO TAILS OR A THIRD BALL . BUT THEY REPRESENT A CERTAIN EFFORT . AT THIS POINT A GIVEN SPECIES BLOWS ITS CREATIVE WAD .

I MAKE OUT AN AGENDA . WHICH I STUDY TO SEE WHAT'S NEXT ON THE AGENDA . PAY THE WATER BILL . I PEEL THE MISSUS OFF THE RUG . SLAP ON A RECORD . AND UNDERGO A FOXTROT . LET US CELEBRATE MY PET . WHILE YOUTH LINGERS . AND IDEAS FLOW . I MIX UP A COOL CUBA LIBRE . WE TOSS OFF A NIGHTCAP . OUT JUMPS MY PECKER LIKE A CORKSCREW . I'LL BANG OFF THE MISSUS ON THE LAZY SUSAN . NOW THERE'S AN IDEA . I KNOW WHEN I'VE GOT IT . I KNOW WHEN I'VE HAD IT .

I CAN FEEL IT SLIPPING AWAY . ME LITTLE SIGNS . I'VE BEEN WORKING ON THE WHISKERS .

I ENTER UPON STUDIES . STRUCTURAL DEMOLITION . HOT NIGHTS IN THE LAB OVER A BUNSEN BURNER . IN PRELIMINARY TESTS . COMBUST WHISKERS . TERMINATE STUDIES .

LOST A TOOTH IN A SILVER SPRUCE .

I DON'T CARE . A CERTAIN I DON'T CARE HAS GONE DOWN THROUGH THE PROPER CHANNEL . THE BACKBONE . PRIDE OF THE VERTEBRATES . AND ROOTED ITSELF IN THE STUFF OF LIFE . CARBON . ATOM TURNS TO ATOM AND SAYS . I DON'T CARE .

DID YOU SEE THAT . THINGS ARE MOVING OUT ALREADY . DUST . LINT . FURNITURE . THE PORTABLE SAUNA . EVERYTIME I LOOK AWAY THEY MOVE TOWARD THE DOOR . ALL CREATURE COMFORTS . ME TOO . EVERYTIME I LOOK AWAY I MOVE TOWARD THE DOOR . WONDER WHERE I GO .

A SPECIES IN EXTREMITIES . AT ODDS WITH ITS ENVIRONMENT . A CLASSIC CASE . MUTATE . OR FACE YOUR FATE . DOWN IN THE DNA THEY'RE BURNING THE MIDNIGHT OIL .

67

AND THERE IS THAT BEAVER THAT KNOWS IT'S ALL OVER BUT THE SHOUTING . THIS DUDE IS A HEAVYWEIGHT . THE RAT WHO STANDS PAT WHILE THEY PLAY NEARER MY GOD TO THEE . AND THEN GOES DOWN . VERY RARE . HE IS ROMMEL RETREATING ACROSS AFRICA . HE IS VON STROHEIM SHOOTING GREED .

I CAN SEE A BEAVER WHO CAN RISE ABOVE IT ALL . **RODANTUM AMPHIBIUM SUPER MUNDANUM** . CHARACTERIZED BY ITS INCREASED CAPACITY FOR HOT AIR . HERETOFORE THE BEAVER HARDLY HELD HOT AIR ENOUGH TO KEEP ITS HEAD ABOVE THE WATER . NOW IT FLOATS ABOVE THE TREE TOPS LIKE A BUBBLE IN THE AIR .

I'LL BE DAMNED . NOT A GHOST OF A PREMONITION . SMACK DAB IN THE MIDDLE OF THE NIGHT . THE MISSUS . IN THE MOON . ATOP THE DAM . LITTER IN A RING AROUND . ALL OF THEM SQUEALING . SHE RAISES HER PAW . IN HER PAW A HAZEL SWITCH . WHACK . ON THEIR BACKS . OFF THEY GO SQUEALING . ONE OF THEM TURNS . BEGS . WHACK . OFF IT GOES SQUEALING . NOT A MOMENT'S HESITATION . SLINGS A ROCK AROUND HER NECK . HOLDS HER NOSE . AND INTO THE POOL . INTO THE MOONLIGHT . BOBBING .

PHYLOGENETICALLY . MY PET . IT'S PART OF OUR TRADITION TO LEAVE A SINKING SHIP . NOT TO GO DOWN .

I WADE OVER THE MISSUS . THERE SHE STICKS . IN THE MUD . LIKE A STICK IN THE MUD . TAIL LIKE A BOARD . BEAVER BOARD . EXCUSE ME . THERE YOU HAVE IT . **RODANTUS CATATONIUS** .

LIKE A FLASH IT SEIZES ME . THE LITTER . OUT THERE . IN THE DARK . IN THE WORLD . DON'T PANIC MY PET . I'LL PULL IT OFF AGAIN . I'LL BRING IT ALL HOME AGAIN . THE BROOD . THE BLOOM . THE BACON . I'LL TRANSVERSE THEIR HYPOTENUSE . I'LL STRIKE OUT AT AN OBTUSE ANGLE AND INTERSECT THE LITTLE BUGGERS ONE BY ONE . ALL IT TAKES IS PLAIN GEOMETRY . ONCE WE BEAVERS SET A COURSE THERE'S NO DEVIATION .

I STARE AT THE MISSUS . RIGHT INTO HER EYE . IT'S DEEP . HER EYE REFLECTS MY EYE . I HOLD MY BREATH AND LOOK HER IN THE EYE . AND THINK OF PYTHAGORAS .

A LITTLE RAIN IS FALLING . AN EYE IS WEEPING . A DAM BREAKS . A TEAR FALLS . IT FALLS OUT OF MY EYE . I CAN SEE IT IN HER EYE . NEITHER OF US BAT AN EYE .

NOW THE MISSUS IS NOT POPULAR WITH THE FEMINIST SET . SHE WAS AN OLD FASHIONED BEAVER . RAISED ON THE PRESERVE . RELIGIOUS BACKGROUND . CREATIVE ASPIRATIONS . OFF TO A SMALL WOMEN'S COLLEGE . FIRST TIME AWAY FROM HOME . USED TO WRITE POETRY AT NIGHT AND EAT IT IN THE MORNING .

PICTURE HIM THEN . SHARP TEETH . CRITICAL MIND . PLANS . DREAMS . THEY WOULD BUILD SOMETHING TOGETHER .

OFF UPSTATE INTO A PARADISE OF BROOKS AND RILLS . SMALL COMMUNITY . GOOD WOOD ON THE BANK .

GOT A CARD IN THE MORNING MAIL . DEAR SIR . REGARDING YOUR STRUCTURE . WE REGRET TO INFORM YOU THAT THERE'S NOTHING ON THE SHELVES YOU WANT . WE ARE SEARCHING THE STACKS . I PERSONALLY AM SEARCHING THE STACKS . I SEARCH THE STACKS EVERY EVENING AFTER WE SHUT OUR LITTLE DOORS .

I FLIP OVER THE CARD . PICTURE OF AN EASTER BUNNY . A BLUE EGG . **P E A C E** . IN RED LETTERS . A PIECE . HMM . SMALL PRINT . EASTER BUNNY . VITAL STATISTICS . SEVEN . FOURTEEN . TWENTY ONE . I SAY . FUCK IT ALL . SHE THINKS I'M A RABBIT .

WILL SET THAT RIGHT . I WRITE . I'M A BIT OF A BADGER AT BOTTOM . A WEASEL ON UP . TWO RAT TEETH . A HARELIP . AND THIS WET BRICKBAT KEEPS FOLLOWING ME AROUND . THROUGH THE COWSLIPS . AND THE COW PADDIES . I'M THREE BY SIX IN ROUND FIGURES . IN FLEXUS . SIX BY NINE . IN EXTENSIO . NINE BY THIRTY FOUR . IN A WORD . YOURS . TRULY .

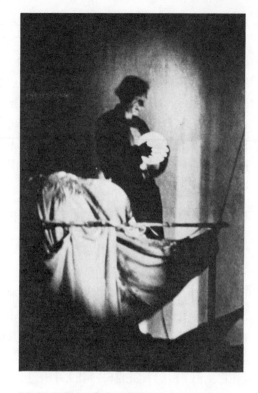

YEARS LATER WHEN B.BEAVER WAS A WINO ON 2ND AVENUE HE DECIDED TO WRITE HIS MEMOIRS ON AN OLD CHECKBOOK . HE WROTE THE FIRST CHECK . PAY TO THE ORDER OF GOD . THROUGH THE NOSE . AND THE SECOND . PAY TO BEARER . RETROACTIVELY . THE WAGES OF LOVE . AND ANOTHER TEAR CAME TO HIS EYE LIKE THE ONE IN THE STORY . EAT YOUR HEART OUT DIMITRI TIOMKIN .

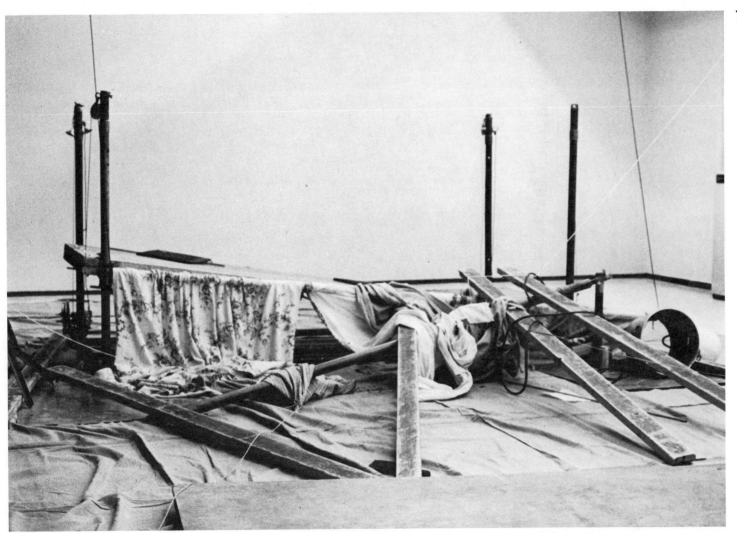

THE SHAGGY DOG ANIMATION

for **RUTH MALECZECH** AND **BILL RAYMOND**

Mabou Mines premièred THE SHAGGY DOG ANIMATION at the New
York Shakespeare Festival's Public Theater in 1978. Written and
conceived for the stage by Lee Breuer. Produced and realized by Mabou
Mines.

Cast .JoAnne Akalaitis, Clove Galilee, Ruth
Maleczech, Gregory Mehrten, Jessie Nelson,
Frederick Neumann, Terry O'Reilly, Bill
Raymond, Linda Wolfe

Set designs based on the concepts of Gordon Matta-Clark

Puppets Rose and John . . . . . . Linda Wolfe
Rose's Living Loft . . . . Don and Rebecca Christensen
Stereo and Street Scene . . . . . . Alison Yerxa
Cloud . . . . Julie Archer
Performance Stage . . . . Jerry Mayer and John Pynchon Holms
Elevator . . . . April Webster
Mirror Wall . . . . L.B. Dallas
Cutting Table . . . . Robin Thomas
Brass Bed . . . . David Hardy
Sound Design and Mix . . . . Robin Thomas
Percussion Riffs . . . . Don Christensen
Lighting. . . . . Robin Thomas and Alison Yerxa
Costume: First Act . . . . Sally Rosen
                Second Act . . . . . . Jeanne Button
                Third Act . . . . Dru-Ann Chuckran
Technical Direction . . . . Robin Thomas
Stage Manager . . . . L.B. Dallas

DEAR JOHN . GOOD BYE . NOW DON'T LAUGH . DON'T CRY . I'M
LEAVING YOU . TO PURSUE . PERFECTION . OR DIE . NO LIE .

JOHN . SINCE THE NIGHT I LEFT . THAT NOTE FOR YOU . ON THE RUG .
UNDER MY FLEA COLLAR . I'VE KEPT MY SILENCE . MY SILENCE AND
MY SPACE WERE MY BELONGINGS . I TRAVELED WITH THEM . I PACKED
THEM CAREFULLY . AND LAID THEM OUT WHERE I COULD . BECAUSE OF
WRINKLES . BECAUSE OF MILDEW .

WHY DO I CONTACT YOU . NOW . OUT OF THE BLUE . OH . WHO
KNOWS . MAYBE I CAN HELP YOU . FAT CHANCE . NO SILLY . IT'S PART
OF MY WORK . HERE . AT THE INSTITUTE .

JOHN . HEY JACK . LISTEN TO THIS . I STILL WANT TO LICK YOUR
EYES . I HAVE TO DEAL WITH THAT . IF I DON'T . DEAL WITH THAT . I
COULD HAVE A POWER FAILURE .

EYES .

I REMEMBER THE FIRST TIME I LAID EYES ON YOU . YOU WERE
ACROSS THE ROOM . TALKING TO MY MOTHER'S MASTER . I SAW A
SPACE AT YOUR FEET . BETWEEN YOUR FEET THERE WAS A SPACE MY
SIZE . I CREPT INTO IT .
IN THE DEAD OF NIGHT THE SUN WAS OUT . AT ITS ZENITH OVER YOU .
THROWING YOUR FORESHORTENED SHADOW LIKE A SWEET DARK
MELTING OF YOU DOWN . THAT WAS MY PLACE . I KNEW MY PLACE . I

KNEW HOW BIG I WAS . I WAS THE DIMENSION OF THE SHADOWY
SPACE FROM ONE SHOE TO THE OTHER . DOWN THERE AT YOUR FEET .

YOU LEFT . I WAS NUMB . I PISSED ON THE FLOOR . JOHN . I WAS IN
LOVE WITH YOU .

I WAS DESPERATE TO SEE YOU AGAIN . I WHINED ALL NIGHT AND
SUCKED MYSELF OFF . MY MOTHER THOUGHT I WAS UNCLEAN . SHE
GAVE ME BATHS . IT RAINED . I DESPAIRED .

YOU CAME BACK . YOU CAME FOR ME . YOU GATHERED ME UP . TOOK
ME . FOR WHAT I WAS . YOUR OWN . YOU CARRIED ME HOME IN YOUR
BOMBER JACKET . INCLEMENT WEATHER CHOSE FOR US A TRYSTING
PLACE . I WENT IN A DREAM . AND DREAMED OF A LIFE NEVER
FARTHER FROM YOU THAN YOUR WHISTLE .

PUPPY LOVE . I MISS YOU . WHEN I CLOSE MY EYES . BUT ALL YOU DO
IS FEED ME LIES . YOU RUN AROUND ALL OVER TOWN . YOU TIE ME
UP . YOU PUT ME DOWN .

AT HOME I THREW MYSELF AT YOU AND PRESSED MY WET NOSE INTO
YOUR ARMPIT . YOU DROPPED ME LIKE A HOT POTATO . DOWN . GIRL .
YOU SAID . AFTER YOU'D READ THE TRAINING MANUAL . YOU DROPPED
THE GIRL . AND TOOK TO SNAPPING YOUR FINGERS .

WHAT DID I EVER DO SO BAD . TO MAKE YOU MAD . BLOW MY MIND .
DON'T BLOW MY COVER . PUPPY LOVER .

78 YOU TOOK AS WELL TO LEAVING ME . ANOTHER OF YOUR LESSONS .
DOUBTLESS . TO ME . INCOMPREHENSIBLE . AS ALWAYS . AND MORE
THE LESSON FOR IT .

YOU WOULD CHANGE MY WATER AND GO . AND ALONE . I VANISHED .
I'D LOOK IN MY WATER AND SEE NOTHING . BUT AN ANIMAL .
SPOOKED . CRAZY .

I WAS OUT OF SIGHT . JOHN . GOD DAMN YOU . I WAS OUT OF MIND .
JACK . GOD FUCK YOU . I WAS NOTHING . MORE . THAN A CATEGORY OF
BEHAVIOR . MS. BEHAVIOR . IN MY PAIN I ATE THE PLANTS . IN MY
DESPAIR I LAID A TURD ON LESLIE'S CARPET .

LESLIE . IF YOU ARE WITHIN REACH . OR EARSHOT . IF YOU CAN HEAR
ME . OR RECEIVE ME . SOMEHOW . I'M NOT SORRY LESLIE . NOT FOR
ANYTHING . YOU SUCK . LESLIE .

DEAR JOHN . I THOUGHT I WOULD NEVER SEE YOU AGAIN . I PEERED
FROM THE WINDOW LEDGE AS CROW FROM GRAVESTONE . THE STREET
WAS VOID OF YOU . I RIPPED THE SCREEN . AND LEAPED ONTO THE FIRE
ESCAPE . CREAMING THE BEGONIA . I'M NOT SORRY .

IT WAS RAINING . AND SO HOT . THUNDERS ROLLED BY LIKE ASHCANS
KICKED DOWN AN ALLEY . LIGHTENING TARGETED THE PASSERS BY .
WIND GUSTS OF WATER DROPS MACHINE GUNNED THEM DOWN .

I WENT BANANAS . I SAT IN THE RAIN AND HOWLED UP THE AVENUE .
WATER POURED OUT OF MY MOUTH LIKE A DRAIN . I WAS BLIND TO MY
FATE . I WAS DEAF TO THE MUSIC . AND THEN I HEARD . THE MUSIC
OF MY SISTERS .

AT ALL LEVELS . ON FIRE ESCAPES LINING THE AVENUES . IN
WINDOWS . ON BALCONIES AND ROOFS . THE DOGS OF THE CITY SANG
WITH ME . WE SISTERS . WE BITCHES . WE PRISONERS OF LOVE .

I WAS NOT A PRISONER ALONE . I WAS NOT AFRAID ALONE . NOT IN
LOVE ALONE . NOT ALONE ALONE . I WAS WITH MY SISTERS . WE
GIRLS . HOW WE HOWLED . HOW WE LANCED WITH THE SPUR OF SONG
THE BOIL OF OUR AFFLICTION .

THEN THERE YOU WERE . AT THE DOOR . YOU KNEELED . YOU TOUCHED
ME . AND WITH A LITTLE WHINE I ROLLED OVER ONTO MY BACK . AND
WAS TRANSFORMED INTO ANOTHER SPECIES OF BEING . A LOVED ONE .

I LICKED YOUR FEET . I MOANED . I PRANCED . PIROUETTED . TAIL
BETWEEN MY LEGS I JUMPED OVER THE CASTRO CONVERTIBLE . JOHN .
DO YOU REMEMBER . THAT WAS THE NIGHT I DANCED FOR YOU .

YOU WATCHED ME . TURNING ON YOUR HEELS . YOUR EYES TWINKLED .
OBSERVED THUS . I BECAME . YOU MADE ME . RIDICULOUS . I DIDN'T
CARE . I WAS A FOOL . LOVE'S FOOL . DANCING . A CLOWN AT HER
DEVOTIONS . LOOK AT HER GO . YOU SAID TO THAT PERSON YOU WERE
WITH . THAT FEMALE PERSON . LESLIE .

YOU SAID COME . I CAME TO YOU . FORMALLY . CLASSICALLY . LIKE A
WORM . WORMING MY WAY TO YOU ON MY BACK . YOU SAT ON THE
BED . YOU KICKED OFF A SHOE . I TOOK YOUR FOOT BETWEEN MY
INCISORS AND MY EYE TEETH AND SLIPPED MY TONGUE BETWEEN
YOUR TOES . YOU HAD A LITTLE SORE . ATHLETE'S FOOT . I TASTED
IT . I LOVED YOUR IMPERFECTIONS . JOHN . YOU TURNED ME ON . MAN .
YOU MADE MY TAIL WAG . BABY .

80 IN THE DEAD OF NIGHT I STOLE FROM MY BLANKET TO THE FOOT OF
YOUR BED . THE SHEET WAS THROWN BACK . I COULD SEE YOUR
COCK . THAT FEMALE PERSON WAS EXPOSED AS WELL .

WHAT ABOUT HER WAS REPUGNANT TO ME . HER SPECIEL SECURITY
PERHAPS . OH JOHN . OUR BODIES ARE MADE FOR EACH OTHER .
LESLIE WAS WONT TO DECLARE AT APPROPRIATE MOMENTS . AN
OPINION I FELT TO BE TOTALLY SUBJECTIVE AND PATENTLY UNTRUE .

ATREMBLE . LEST SHE AWAKEN . I CREPT UP BETWEEN YOUR LEGS .
CLOSED MY EYES . AND GAVE YOU A BLOW JOB .

PHYSICAL LOVE WAS ALWAYS SOMETHING OF A PROBLEM . I THINK WE
CAN ADMIT THAT NOW . OUR LIFE IN BED WAS NEVER SERENE . WE
BLAMED IT ON DISTRACTIONS . THE TELEPHONE . DEBTS . POLLUTION .
FLEAS . JOHN . BE IT EVER SO BELATED LET ME HERE AND NOW
APOLOGIZE . I TRIED EVERYTHING . POWDERS . SPRAYS . THE COLLAR .
REMEMBER THAT NASTY RASH I GOT FROM THE COLLAR .
INCIDENTALLY . I'M CERTAIN NOW IT WAS A FLEA THAT WOKE UP
LESLIE .

YOU KNOW THE REST JOHN . HOW SHE KICKED ME . THE CUNT . HOW
SHE RAISED HER VOICE TO ME . CALLED ME BAD DOG . YOU THOUGHT
IT WAS PRETTY FUNNY . A LOAD OF YUCKS .

ME . LICKING THE COME OFF MY NOSE AND TRYING TO CRAWL UNDER
THE MATTRESS . REMEMBER HOW THE BITCH LOCKED ME IN THE
TOILET . IN SOLITARY CONFINEMENT . PURINA AND WATER . I GOT HER
THOUGH . YOU KNOW HOW I GOT HER JOHN . SHE WAS THE DEVIL .

NOW JOHN I KNOW YOU DON'T AGREE WITH ME ABOUT THE DEVIL . I'M
AWARE WE HAVE CONFLICTING RELIGIOUS VIEWS . I CAN SAY ONLY

THAT I HAVE BEEN . INFORMED . MY BODY INFORMS ME OF EVIL . MY HACKLES RISE . MY THROAT CONSTRICTS . MY EARS FLATTEN . AND MY LIP CURLS . THIS IS THE TELEPATHY OF GOD . I AM GOD'S RECEIVER . BECAUSE I AM A GOOD DOG . I AM GOD'S HOWITZER . BECAUSE I AM A GOOD DOG . I AM GOD'S NOSE .

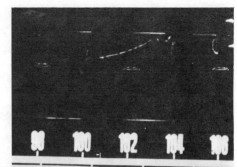

I SMELL THE DEVIL IN A SAUCER OF MILK . IN THE WARM SPOT ON THE CUSHION OF A CHAIR . I HEAR A YOWL IN THE MIDNIGHT HOUR . LITTLE CLAWS AGAINST THE WINDOW SCREEN . A PURRING IN THE LITTER GREEN . SHE'S PUSSY . JOHN . SHE'S PUSSY PEOPLE .

MY DARLING . MY INNOCENT . I FEAR FOR YOU AS FOR THE BLIND CHILD CROSSING THE NIGHT STREET IN A BLACK SWEATER .

I EMERGED FROM THE BATHROOM A CHANGED DOG . I WAS A DIRTY DOG . A LITTLE SEED WAS GROWING IN MY DIRT . WHAT WAS THE NAME OF THAT SEED . COME ON BABY . WHAT WAS THE NAME OF THAT SEED . HEY JACK . I'M LAUGHING NOW . BUT I WAS PRETTY MAD THEN . WASN'T I .

LATER ON . IN THE WEE HOURS . LESLIE GOT UP FOR A MIDNIGHT SNACK . I STALKED HER TO THE KITCHEN AND FLATTENED MYSELF BETWEEN THE WATER HEATER AND THE WALL . SHE WAS A FREAK FOR LEFTOVERS . THAT NIGHT . IT WAS RAVIOLI .

THE MOON WAS FULL AND RINGING IN THE WINDOWGLASS . ANCIENT POWERS ROSE AND BID FOR ME . BITCHES . GREY AND BLEAK AS STONE ABOVE THE TIMBERLINE . AND AS EPHEMERAL AS FOG . MY BITCHES . MY WOLVES . MY CERBERI .

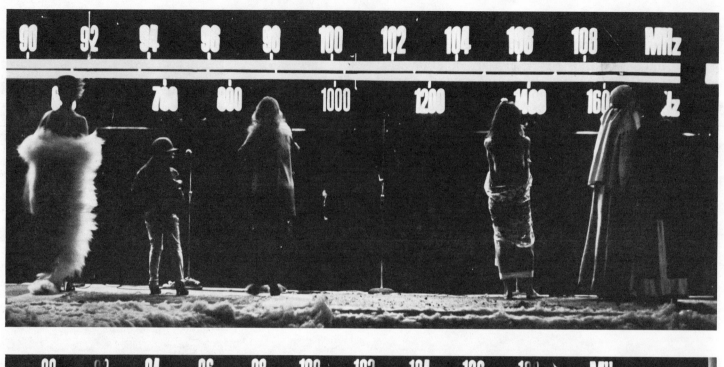

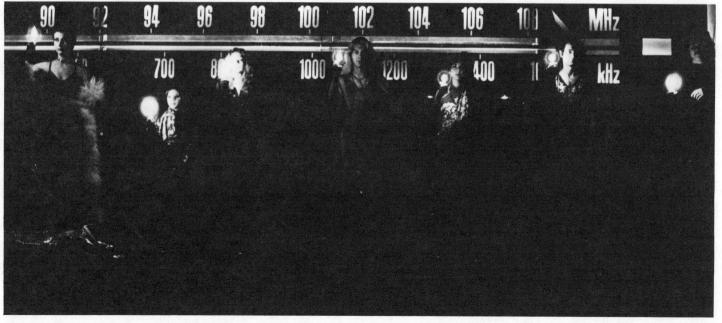

I COULD DO IT . I COULD DO IT . I COULD GO FOR HER THROAT . WITH A HIDEOUS SNARL I POUNCED ONTO THE DRAINBOARD AND SNAPPED A RAVIOLI RIGHT OUT OF HER HAND . SHE FROZE . WE WERE EYEBALL TO EYEBALL . I ATE THEM ALL . AND CURLED MY LIP . AND FARTED .

IN THAT MOMENT THERE BEGAN FOR ME A SECRET CONTEST WITH REALITY . IN THE FACE OF THE EVIDENCE OF MY SENSES . COUNTER TO THE EMPIRICALLY PROVED . HEEDLESS OF HISTORY . DESPITE PSYCHOLOGY . AGAINST ODDS . ALL ODDS . AGAINST REASONS . ALL REASONS . I ENTERED A SECRET COMPETITION TO WIN YOU . A CLOSED COMPETITION WITH MY FATE . AGAINST REASON I ENLISTED FAITH . AND IN SUPPORT OF FAITH I CULTIVATED MADNESS . FROM THENCE FORTH UNTIL I SAID GOOD BYE . JOHN GREED . I WAS YOUR FAITHFUL DOG . YOUR MAD DOG ROSE . I WAS YOUR FAITHFUL DOG . MASTER . UNTIL FAITH WAS BROKEN .

I HAVE TO STOP HERE . NOT BECAUSE I'M THROUGH . BECAUSE I'M CRYING .

IMAGE TRACK

NOW THEN . IN THIS AWE INSPIRING PLACE . FREE FROM TREMBLING . AND UNCHALLENGED BY GHOSTS . YOU PLAY . FOR YOUR DELIVERANCE FROM THE BODY OF YOUR IMAGINATION .

THE CONFIDENTIAL WORD IS . GREED . THE DOG IDENTIFIES . GREED . WITH HER BEDROOM .

84 **I'M CRYING** . TEARDROPS HANG ON MY WHISKERS AND DRIZZLE INTO MY NOSE . I LOOK DUMB . TOO DUMB TO COME IN OUT OF THE RAIN . BUT IN REALITY I'M A LUCKY DOG .

SORROW HAS FOUND A WARP IN MY KARMA AND SENT ME GIFTS FROM A LIFE TO COME . TEAR DUCTS . BEHIND MY HANGDOG EXPRESSION LIES A CAPACITY FOR GRIEF OF ANOTHER KIND . YOUR KIND MASTER DEAR . I'M COMING TO YOU MASTER . UPRIGHT . IN THE SUNLIGHT . UNLESS OF COURSE IT'S ALL AN ILLUSION . AND IN REALITY . I'M COMING FOR YOU . AT MIDNIGHT .

LOOK . I'M WEEPING . LOOK MASTER DEAR . LOVE HAS MADE ME OVER . SIRIUS . MY STAR . MUST BE ASCENDING . UNLESS OF COURSE IT'S ALL AN ILLUSION . AND IN REALITY . I'M SLIPPING . DOWN TO A CROCODILE .

HOT DOG . LESLIE SPLIT TO ORLANDO FLORIDA . FOUR WEEKS CLASS C CONTRACT AT THE RAINBOW RIALTO DINNER SHOWCASE . TWENTY FIVE MINUTES FROM DISNEY WORLD . REMEMBER JOHN HOW HER AGENT CALLED AND SAID SHE WAS TOO OLD FOR DOROTHY . BUT THEY NEEDED A WICKED WITCH OF THE WEST .

HERE COMES THE VISUALS .

CHECK THAT . A HOBART 700 SPEED QUEEN DISHWASHER WITH POT SCRUBBING ACTION .

LOOK AT THE DETAIL . MAKES YOU WANT TO GIVE YOURSELF THE REST OF THE NIGHT OFF .

WHAT I LIKE ABOUT THIS PART . ROSE . IS ITS OBJECTIVITY . ITS . LOVE OBJECT . TIVITY .

COOL AS A CUCUMBER . LOOK AT THAT CUCUMBER .

HOWARD HUGHES HAD ONE THAT LOOKED LIKE HEDY LAMARR . THE GOSSIP GOES THAT HE . . HE . . . FORGET IT .

THOSE WERE THE DAYS MON PETIT CHOU . MY PORK CHOP . MY LITTLE
DOCTOR ROSS MILK BONE . MELLOW DAYS . DOG DAYS . DO YOU
RECALL OUR WALKS . WE'D STOP FOR BRUNCH IN THE WEST VILLAGE .
ONE OF THOSE CONTINENTAL JOBIES WITH TABLES ON THE SIDE
WALKS . I'D CURL UP WITH MY CHEEK ON YOUR HUARACHIS . YOU .
HAVING THE ASPARAGUS OMELET WITH WHITE WINE . ME HAVING THE
FRENCH FRIES . YOU WERE WATCHING YOUR LOVE HANDLES . JOHN .
YOU WERE ANXIOUS .

ROSE . WAKE UP . WE'VE GO TO GO
OUT . NOBODY'S GOING TO WALK
US ROSE . ALL OUR BEST FRIENDS
ARE DEAD TO THE WORLD .

ROSE . WAKE UP . IT'S TWELVE .
IT'S COLD . THE CLOSET IS BARE .
WE'VE NOTHING TO WEAR . BUT WE
.DON'T CARE . 'CAUSE WE GOT
HAIR . ROSE . PUT ON THE DOG .

86 AND CRUISING WITH YOU UP FIFTH AVENUE . AT TWILIGHT . INTO THE EAST SIXTIES . ALL THOSE FANCY LITTLE BREEDS WALKING AROUND . THE LHASA APSO WHO JUST COULDN'T LEAVE YOU ALONE . THAT COCKAPOO . THE ONE THAT BIT MY EAR IN A TERRIBLE SNIT . I WAS NAIVE . YOU'D BEEN HANGING OUT . JOHN . HADN'T YOU . SOCIAL CLIMBING BY THE HYDRANT . YOU'D BEEN HUSTLING THOSE EAST SIXTIES' DOGS .

DEAR JOHN . I UNDERSTOOD YOU IN MY FASHION . JULY WAS FIREWORKS . THE HEAT WAS ON . ME TOO . I SHED MY UNDERCOAT AND GOT HUMPED BY A SALUKI . BY THE NAME OF BROADWAY . YOU WERE HURT . I COULD TELL . AND I PAID . I PAID THE ONLY WAY I COULD IN MY POSITION . I ATE SHIT .

ROSE . YOU'VE COME A LONG WAY . BABY .
BARK .
STAY .

NOW FURNISH THE DOG WITH A SMALL HOUSE OF AN APPROPRIATE DECOR .
A BALL FOR HIGH FLUNG RESOLVE .

FETCH .
GO ON . NOBODY'S LOOKING . THAT'S A GOOD GIRL .
SHAKE .
NOW . TAKE FOUR EXALTED STEPS .
SIT .

PUT ON THE DOG A COLLAR WITH
A TINKLING BELL . THIS CHARMS
THE ANIMALS .

AND YOU REQUIRE WATER IN A
BOWL FOR QUENCHING FIRES .
ALSO SERVICING TO DROWN
REGRETS .

ROSE . YOU NEED A STICK THAT
YOU CAN GNAW DOWN TO A POINT .
THIS WORKS ON WEREWOLVES .
AND FOR PROTECTION FROM THE
OTHER DEMONS WEAR A WHISTLE
PAST THE RANGE OF DEMON EARS .
AND EVERY TIME YOU SEE ONE
CALL YOUR PACK .

AND ROSE . YOUR ACCESSORIES
SHOULD INCLUDE A BONE . TO
BURY . SOMEWHAT LIKE A
HATCHET . AND SOMETHING LIKE
GRIEF .

RESTRAIN THE DOG WITH A LEASH
OF HAIR . PLAIT IT WITH BLACK
HAIR OF PANTHER . WHITE OF
LEOPARD . YELLOW HAIR OF

BENGAL TIGER . CINCH AND KNOT
WITH LION'S MANE . THE BIG
CATS . ALL THE GREAT CATS . AND
THE HIP CATS . ALL THE
BEAUTIES .

THE CONFIDENTIAL WORD IS .
PRIDE . ROSE . CONQUER YOUR
PRIDE .

HOW OFTEN HAD I RACKED MY POOR LITTLE BRAIN . JOHN DEAR . FOR
MISTER HOOK . THE CANINE CONNECTION .

HOW LONG . HAD I LONGED . TO SING THE SONG . THAT PLUGGED YOUR
PRONG . INTO MY SOCKET .

AND THERE IT WAS . SWEETS . KINKY REGGAE . I GUESS NO ONE HAD
EVER EATEN YOUR SHIT BEFORE AND LIKED IT . YOU HAD TO DRAG ME
AWAY FROM THE TOILET . WHICH YOU DIDN'T . YOU HAD TO MUZZLE
MY MOUTH . A THING THAT YOU ABHORRED TO DO . TO YOUR ROSE .
YOUR AMERICAN BEAUTY . POOR JOHN . YOU TURNED INTO A REAL DOG
LOVER .

NOW ROSE I'M GOING TO GIVE YOU
SOME DIRECTIONS . SOUTH .
EAST . WEST . NORTH . AND
CENTER . I'M GOING TO ASK YOU
TO DEAL WITH THE TRADITIONAL
MATERIAL . YOUR STUPIDITY . AND
ITS TRANSMUTATION .

ROSE . CONQUER YOUR PRIDE .
THIS IS AN ACTING PROBLEM .
PICTURE YOURSELF . A DUMMY .

DON'T ASK ME QUESTIONS . I'M
JUST A PROMPTER . LOVE .

HERE WE ARE NOW . AT THE IDEA
OF THE SOUTH . THE COLOR BLUE .
THE PEAR SHAPED . THE SOUND OF
TAPPING . AND THE HEAD OF
PRIDE .

WAKE UP ROSE . THIS IS A GOLDEN
OPPORTUNITY . TO FIX THE
MECHANISM OF YOUR LIFE . CHECK
EACH PIN HINGE . ALL YOU HAVE
TO FIND OUT IS HOW EVERYTHING'S
ATTACHED . PICTURE YOURSELF AS
AN OBJECT OF ATTACHMENT .

WHAT'S THE MATTER . ARE YOU
SCARED . YOU'RE AT HOME .

THE DOG IDENTIFIES THE HEAD OF
PRIDE WITH HER VERY OWN
BATHROOM . WHAT ARE YOU
SCARED OF . OH I KNOW . YOUR
MIND . WELL WHAT CAN I SAY .
KNOCK ON WOOD . SEE . NO
PROBLEM .

WELL . WHAT IS IT NOW . OH . I
KNOW WHAT YOU'RE THINKING
ROSE . YOU'RE GOING TO LOOK LIKE
A DUMMY .

IT CAME TOGETHER . YEAH . IN VENICE . IT STILL TAKES MY BREATH AWAY . VENICE AND YOU . LESLIE HAD LANDED THAT BROMO PROMO . I CAN STILL SEE YOUR FACE WHEN SHE CALLED . WHAT A TRIP SHE LAID DOWN . COME TO VENICE . ON ME . V.I.P. DON'T BRING THE DOG . YOU SAT DOWN LIKE A ZOMBIE . TURNED ON THE MIDNIGHT SPECIAL . AND SQUEEZED YOUR SEA AND SKI . IT WAS A TIME OF DECISION .

THAT SUNDAY THE TICKET CAME . WE LAY ON THE RUG . MY NOSE IN YOUR NAVEL . WATCHING THE DOLPHINS AND THE JETS . YOU WERE FLIPPING POPCORN INTO YOUR MOUTH . YOU MISSED . A POPCORN ROLLED ONTO YOUR CHEST . BANKED ON A RIB . AND DROPPED INTO YOUR HOLE . BIRDIE . I SAID . AND LICKED IT OUT . THEN I LICKED UP YOUR STOMACH ALL ALONG THE BUTTER DRIPS . IT WAS FOURTH DOWN AND GOAL TO GO . YOU SAID . COME FLY WITH ME .

WHAT A SCENE AT THE AIRPORT . FIRST THEY WANTED TO SEE MY PAPERS . SHOTS . LICENSE . THE WORKS . THEN THEY WEIGHED ME . I WAS OVER THE LIMIT . WHICH MEANT I WAS NOT A LAP DOG . WHICH MEANT . I WAS BAGGAGE .

I GUESS IT'S ALWAYS LIKE THAT WHEN YOU ACT IMPULSIVELY . THE PEAKS AND THE PITS ALL LUMPED TOGETHER . AND LIKE ALL IMPULSIVE MOMENTS IT WAS COSTLY . FORTY FIVE DOLLARS FOR A FLYING KENNEL . SURCHARGE . AND THREE TWENTY FIVE FOR DOGGIE TRANQS . WE HAD TO CASH IN YOUR FIRST CLASS TICKET AND TAKE THE RED EYE SPECIAL . GOODBYE FIRST RUN FEATURE AND NAPA VALLEY CHAMPAGNE . LOVE IN FLIGHT WENT HALF ECONOMY AND HALF AIR FREIGHT .

IT CAME TOGETHER . YEAH . ME AND MY MOVIE . WE WENT INTO PRODUCTION . ALL MY LINES CAME TRUE . IT LOOKED LIKE A WINNER . ALL THE MOVES WERE THE RIGHT ONES . AND THE CLOSEUPS WERE TIGHT ONES . I LOVED ME . LOVING YOU .

BUT THEN . WHEN . AT THE PHOENIX STOPOVER YOU GOT ME OUT OF THE CAGE AND BROUGHT A PAPER CUP OF WATER . AND WHEN IT WAS CHAMPAGNE TO ME . MY MIND WAS CLEANSED OF DOUBT . IN THE FAITH THAT MY HEART COULD DO ANYTHING . AND THE CARPING OF MY SOUL BLEW OFF . ACROSS THE RUNWAY . IN A NINETY TWO DEGREE WAFT WITH LESS THAN FIVE PER CENT HUMIDITY .

I TOOK A PISS ON A DOTTED WHITE LINE . THAT STRETCHED THROUGH THE MOONLIGHT INTO ETERNITY . THAT IS . IN A MANNER OF SPEAKING . MY MANNER OF SPEAKING . I MADE A TERRITORIAL CLAIM ON ETERNITY FOR TWO . JOHN I SAID . PISS ON IT TOO .

WE DISEMBARKED . AND I THOUGHT I HEARD THE VOICE OF DOOM . YOU WERE BEING PAGED . A MESSAGE FROM LESLIE ON THE WHITE COURTESY PHONE . ON LOCATION IN TOLUCA LAKE . SHOOTING ALL NIGHT . THE KEY IS IN THE CACTUS PLANT . FEED THE GUPPY . I WAS WRONG . IT WAS THE VOICE OF REPRIEVE .

THE SAND WAS PUCK MARKED LIKE A QUILT . AND WARM LIKE A BODY . YOU SMOOTHED BACK MY EARS AND CUPPED MY FACE . MY MOUTH OPENED . AND MY EYES CLOSED . YOU SAID ROSE . I SAID LET'S DROP SOME ACID .

IT WAS TWO A.M. IN VENICE . AND EVERYONE WAS HAVING THEIR LAST SALAD OF THE NIGHT . EXCEPT THE FRUITARIANS . WHO WERE HAVING APRICOT NECTAR . WE WENT DOWN TO THE WATER SEEKING SECLUSION .

WE BREATHED TOGETHER . I . SLOW LIKE YOU AWHILE . THEN YOU TRIED PANTING LIKE ME . TILL YOU HYPERVENTILATED AND HAD TO SIT DOWN . I RAN A FIGURE EIGHT AROUND THE SQUASH COURT . THEN I DUG A ONE BY TWO BY THREE FOOT HOLE . WHAT ELSE COULD I DO . I WAS DELIRIOUS . IT WAS ALL A DREAM AGAIN . I WAS IN YOUR BOMBER JACKET AGAIN . I SLIPPED OUT OF MY COLLAR . YOU TOOK OFF YOUR PANTS . A WAKI LUA LANI KALOA KALUA MOON SURFED OVER US . AS WE LAY DOGGO .

92 OH JOHN . JOHN . IT WAS A NIGHT OF MIRACLES . I'D NEVER BEEN SO
CLOSE TO YOU . OUT IN THE AIR . I'D NEVER SMELLED YOU IN THE
AURA OF THE STARLIGHT . AND THE SEAWEED . NEVER FELT YOUR
THROAT BEAT . LIKE THE CLAVES . TO THE CONGA . OF MY HEART .

YOU WERE A RHAPSODY . YOU MOVED MY SOUL . MOVED IT RIGHT
BACK THROUGH TIME . AND I KNEW I HAD KNOWN YOU IN ANOTHER
LIFE . AND LOVED YOU IN ANOTHER LIFE . AND LOST .

AND I HELD YOU TILL I ALMOST FAINTED IN YOUR ARMS . LEST YOU'D
SLIP AWAY . AS BEFORE . FORWARD IN TIME . INTO INTERIORS . INTO
CLOTHES AND LANGUAGE . INTO YOUR DUMB SELF . AND NEVER
KNOW . THAT I KNEW YOU . FOR MY OWN TRUE BREED .

AND I LICKED YOUR BEAUTIFUL FACE CLEAN OF SALT . I LICKED BACK
THROUGH YOUR FACES . THE ANIMATIONS . OF YOU . THE POWER .
THAT HAS FOREVER OVERPOWERED ME . I LICKED YOUR FACE TILL
YOUR NOSE TURNED BLACK . AND YOUR EYES MOVED GENTLY TO THE
SIDE . AND BECAME SO DARK AND ROUND . THAT A SPECK OF WHITE
COULD NOT BE SEEN . AND I TRUSTED YOU . YOU WERE MY KEEPER .
JOHN . YOU WERE MY BEST FRIEND . FUCK ME . I SAID . YOU SAID .
HOW . I THOUGHT ABOUT IT .

DO YOU REALLY WANT TO KNOW . SAID I .

WELL . JUST A MINUTE . LET ME GET MY AXE .

THE WORD IS **CUT OFF** . THE DOG
RECOGNIZES HER DOG HOUSE . IN
THE FORM OF HER OWN INTERIOR
DECORATION . SHE STARTS TO
SHATTER HER ILLUSIONS .

YOU'LL LOOK INTO MY EYES . AS IF I WERE YOUR MIRROR . AND FROM REFLECTION TO REFLECTION WE'LL LEAP . LIKE SPARKS OVER A GAP . YOU'LL STAND STONE STILL TILL YOUR VISION CLEARS . SO CLEAR YOU CAN SEE AN ATOM . AND YOU'LL FEEL ME WASH DOWN YOUR BODY INTO YOUR LEGS LIKE WAVES . AND YOU WILL GATHER LIKE A CURRENT IN MY EYE . AND MAKE IT TREMBLE .

YOU'LL SHIVER AS THE MAGIC OF THE AIR COMES DOWN TO REST ON YOU WITH A GLOW LIKE SULPHUR . AND A HALO OF WHITE MOTHS . WITHOUT MOVING YOU'LL BE MOVING . IN A TINY DANCE . YOUR SKIN WILL ASK FOR ME . AS MY EYE ASKS TO LOOK AT YOU . AND EACH TO EACH OTHER . WILL BE REVEALED .

THE WIND WILL RUFF A CHANNEL IN YOUR FUR AND UP YOUR TAIL WILL FLY JUST LIKE A WING . YOU'LL STRETCH FORWARD IN AN ARC

THIS IS JUST A LITTLE HYPE ME AND THE BOYS WORKED UP . WE GOT R.C. GLUED TO THE DIMMER . HI THERE R.C. WE GOT R.T. PATCHED INTO THE DIGITAL DELAY . THIS BOY CAN REALLY DELAY HIS DIGIT . THIS IS A TAKE . THIS IS A DOUBLE TAKE . THAT'S G.M. ON THE CLAPBOARD . HIT ME AGAIN G.M. THIS IS A HIT .

94 AND FALL TO ME . AND PAWS AROUND EACH OTHER'S NECKS . OUR TONGUES OUT . WE'LL SWAY AND POUR SWEAT AND MOAN IN OUR THROATS . THEN YOU'LL WORK YOU WAY DOWN MY BACK . LIGHTLY . AS UPON AN INSTRUMENT . AND WITH MY HEAD THROWN BACK TO GAZE ON YOU . AT LAST YOU'LL COME AROUND TO ME . I'LL LIFT MY TAIL AND FEEL YOU PAW MY BREASTS . YOU'LL MOUNT ME . THROUGH MY STOMACH . ALL ALONG MY VEINS . YOU'LL SLIP THROUGH MY RIB CAGE UP INTO MY THROAT . TILL I'M A SHEATH OF SKIN OVER A THROBBING . TILL I'M NOTHING BUT YOU . NOT A HEART BEAT . NOT A DROP OF BLOOD . NOT A BREATH OF AIR THAT IS NOT . TRANSPARENT .

THEN YOUR HIND LEGS WILL LEAVE THE GROUND. YOU'RE SO LIGHT I CAN CARRY YOU . WE'LL HEAD UP THE BEACH IN A DOG TROT . OVER THE ROCKS AND THROUGH THE LITTLE POOLS OF WATER . WE'LL PICK UP SOME SPEED . AND HIGHTAIL IT UP A DUNE . WE'LL MAKE THE SAND FLY . YEAH .

WE'LL SLEEP UNDER ROCKS AND EAT ORGANIC GARBAGE . BATHING EACH MORNING AT SUNRISE . BRUSHING OUR TEETH WITH TWIGS . JOHN . WE'LL PAINT OURSELVES ORANGE AND POWDER OURSELVES GOLD . WE'LL BE SADDHUS OF LOVE . AND ON STILL NIGHTS FROM CLIFFS OVER THE WATER WE'LL BALE AT THE SKY TILL IT CRACKS LIKE GLASS . AND BATHED IN THE POWERS THERE RELEASED . OUR BONES WILL RING LIKE BELLS .

TWO WAVES . ONE OF SEA AND ONE OF SKY . WILL CROSS US AT RIGHT ANGLES . AND WORK US LOOSE . AND SET US DRIFTING IN THEIR THRALL . AND AS AN IMAGE IN THE SAND . SUCKED BY AN UNDERTOW . THESE POWERS . TOO STRONG FOR OUR FORMS . WILL START TO CHANGE THEM .

TAKE THAT LINE . AT LAST . YOU'LL . COME AROUND . TO ME .

DID YOU HEAR THE ONE ABOUT THE **95**
RUG . THAT PULLS RIGHT OUT
FROM UNDER YOU . DID YOU HEAR
ABOUT THE SIXTEEN HUNDRED
SQUARE FEET OF RUG . EVERY ONE
OF THEM IN YOUR MOUTH . GET
DOWN .

GET DOWN TO THE GROUND PLAN .
RETAKE . ROMANTIC PEOPLE .

WE'LL PICK UP DISEASES . AND FOAM AT THE MOUTH AND GET THIN .
AND CIVILIZED LIFE WILL SHUN OUR KIND . THEY'LL CALL OUT THE
CATCHERS . BUT WE'LL ESCAPE . PAST SANTA BARBARA . PAST SAN
LUIS OBISBO . PAST GORDA . SPECIAL PEOPLE WILL AID AND ABET US .
ROMANTIC PEOPLE . THEY'LL BLOW US KISSES FROM SPORTS CARS
AND BECKON US TO THEIR BEACH BLANKETS WHERE THEY'LL TOAST
OUR HEALTH IN A TEQUILA SUNRISE RIGHT OUT OF A THERMOS . AND
LADEN WITH GIFTS . A LITTLE COKE . A FEW POTATO CHIPS . WE'LL
TURN OFF INTO THE TREES .

WE'LL LEARN TO CLIMB . AND BUILD A DOG HOUSE IN A REDWOOD
TREE . AND FOREGOING RABBITS WE'LL CONCENTRATE ON BIRDS . AND
THAT TOO WILL PASS . AND WE'LL BECOME VEGETARIANS AND EAT
NEEDLES .

AND ONE DAY WEAK FROM FASTING AND DELIRIOUSLY CONTENT .
WE'LL WANDER RIGHT OFF THE EDGE OF THE MOUNTAIN . ONTO
CLOUDS THAT LIE AGAINST IT LIKE A GLACIER OF DREAMS . AND THERE
AT LAST . YOU'LL SLIP DOWN MY BACK AND TURN AROUND . LIFTING
YOUR HIND LEG OVER . INTO A TIE SO TIGHT OUR HEAT WILL STEAM
THE CLOUDS AWAY . AND THERE WE'LL LIE DOWN ON NOTHING AT
ALL . AND STUDY THE PACIFIC .

JOHN . I CLOSED MY EYES . THAT'S HOW DOGS DO IT . YOU SAID .
WHAT THE FUCK . THIS IS VENICE .

IT CAME TOGETHER . YEAH . ME
AND MY MOVIE . HOW COULD I
FALTER . WITH YOU AS MY LEAD .

I PAID MY ADMISSION . AND SAT IN
A BACK ROW . AND PLAYED WITH
MY YO-YO . AND DUG YOU . JOHN
GREED .

IT CAME TOGETHER . YEAH . ME
AND MY MOVIE . THE STORY WAS
ENDLESS . A REAL SHAGGY DOG .

WE PLAYED IN THE HEATHER .
THEN WE PLAYED STORMY
WEATHER . WE CAME TOGETHER .
YEAH . YOU AND ME . HOG .

96

HELLO JOHN. I THOUGHT I'D STOP
AND SAY HELLO TO YOU FOR A
MINUTE . I WAS JUST SITTING
HERE WONDERING IF I COULD EVER
GO DOWN TO THE WATER AGAIN .
AND I WANTED TO SHARE WITH YOU
MY OBSERVATION . FROM ANOTHER
DISTANCE . A MIDDLE DISTANCE .
THAT THE TIME HAD COME TO TELL
THE WORLD . THAT YOU FUCK DOGS
MAN . YOU FUCK THEM OVER . AND
OVER . AND OVER .

I'LL GET YOU YOU SIX TIT
SUCKER . I'LL SPILL THE BEANS .
I'LL CALL THE A.S.P.C.A. YOU'VE
TAKEN THE BEST YEARS OF MY
LIFE . ON THROUGH FOUR . THAT'S
A PUNCH LINE . I SAID . THAT'S
THE WAY TO END A SHAGGY DOG . I
SAID . PART ONE . I SAID .

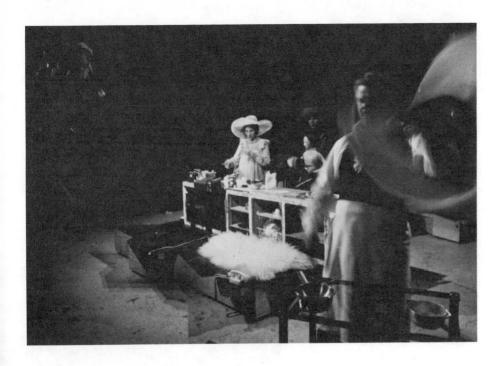

WHAT'S COOKING ROSE . FOOD FOR THOUGHT . PICTURE YOURSELF AS A CREME PUFF . SURE 'NUF . ALL THAT SWEET STUFF . DON'T LAUGH ROSE .

YOUR KNEES COULD TURN TO WATER . **TWO CUPS OF WATER** . AND ON YOUR TONGUE . **A TEASPOON OF SUGAR** . IN YOUR HEART OF HEARTS . **ABOUT A QUARTER POUND OF BUTTER** . PUT IT ALL TOGETHER ROSE . **AND BRING TO A BOIL** .

DON'T LAUGH ROSE . THE WORD IS . **HATE** .

THIS IS THE SAD PART . JOHN . ARE YOU READY FOR THE SAD PART . WE MATURED . EATING SHIT WAS NOT ENOUGH . I COULD SEE THE WRITING ON THE WALL . I WAS LOSING YOU .

DON'T LAUGH ROSE . WE HAVE TO LEARN TO TAKE IT SERIOUSLY . IT'S WHERE WE LIVE . WE CAN SKIP ALL OF THE PLACES SOME OF THE TIME . AND WE CAN SKIP SOME OF THE PLACES ALL OF THE TIME . BUT SOONER OR LATER WE'LL COME TO THE KITCH .

NOW ADD YOUR FLOUR ALL AT ONCE .

ROSE . ADD YOUR FLOUR ALL AT ONCE .

98 THE SCENE WITH LESLIE WAS A TERRIBLE CLICHE . I DON'T WANT TO TALK ABOUT IT . EXCEPT TO SAY . THAT YOU WERE MARVELOUS . AND WHEN YOU TOLD HER HOW YOU'D STOMP HER ASS UNLESS SHE GOT HER NOSE OUT OF THE GUTTER . I WANTED TO CHEER . BUT OF COURSE I HAD TO GO .

WHY DID I HAVE TO GO . I HAD TO GO FOR REASONS JUST OUT OF REACH OF REASONING . TRUST ME . THIS IS MY FAMILIAR GROUND . I HAD TO GO BECAUSE . IT GOES . AND THAT'S THE WAY IT GOES . IT GOES TO THE DOGS .

DO YOU READ ME . JOHN . I'M DOG . I WAS DOMESTICATED SEVENTY THOUSAND YEARS AGO . BEFORE THE HORSE . BEFORE THE WATER BUFFALO . AND WHY . THERE WASN'T ONE GOOD REASON . I COULDN'T CARRY YOU . OR PULL A PLOW . TAKE HUNTING . WHAT A LAUGH . A POINTER POINTING OUT A DINOSAUR . OR A RETRIEVER WITH A MAMMOTH IN ITS MOUTH . NO . THAT WAS JUST A LITTLE MARXIST SHUCK . THAT STUFF ABOUT HISTORICAL NECESSITY .

THE TRUTH IS JOHN THAT WE WERE NEVER FREE . WILD DOGS IN AFRICA . THEY'RE THE MUTATIONS OF THE STOCK . NOT WE . WE PETS . NOT ON YOUR LIFE . WE HAVE NO MYTH OF NOBLE SAVAGERY . THE WILD DIES OFF . BEFORE IT FETCHES SLIPPERS AND THE SUNDAY PAPER . DOGS DON'T DIE . THEY LOVE HONOR AND OBEY .

NOW PADDLE BEAT THE MIXTURE WITH A WOODEN SPOON TILL IT LEAVES THE SIDE OF THE SAUCEPAN AND FORMS A BALL .

ROSE . I BET YOU'RE STARVING . ARE YOU READY FOR THE NEXT STEP . ALRIGHT . ADD YOUR EGGS .

WE ARE THE SECRET SPOUSES OF MANKIND . WE ARE AN IMAGE .
PERCEIVED ONLY IN THE MIRROR OF A MASTER'S EYE . WE ARE A
SELF . IDENTIFIED ONLY BY SELFLESSNESS . WE ARE THE LAWFUL
WEDDED SPECIES OF THE RACE . FOR WE ARE NOTHING . BUT A
SPECIES OF DEVOTION . AND DEVOTION TO ANOTHER ANIMAL IS THE
TEMPTATION OF THE FLESH TO KILL THE SOUL .

GOING TO THE DOGS IS CHOOSING PAIN FOREVER .

BUTTER A LARGE PASTRY SHEET . NOW FIT
YOUR PASTRY BAG WITH A ONE HALF INCH
PLAIN TUBE AND FILL WITH PATE A CHOU .
PIPE OUT EIGHTEEN OR SO PUFFS ABOUT THE
SIZE OF A WALNUT AND ONE INCH HIGH
LEAVING SPACE AROUND EACH PUFF FOR
EXPANSION .

BRUSH THE TOPS OF THE PUFFS WITH ONE EGG
MIXED WITH TWO TABLESPOONS LIGHT
CREAM . TO ENHANCE THEIR COMPLEXION .
THEN POP PUFFS IN OVEN . BAKE AT FOUR
HUNDRED DEGREES .

GOD FUCK YOU . JOHN YOU DIDN'T CALL . YOU DIDN'T WRITE . WHO WERE YOU . DOG LOVER . TWO MONTHS AFTER HOW COULD I REMEMBER . WE HAVE SHORT MEMORIES . YOU SEE . WE'RE NOT ELEPHANTS .

I KNEW YOU LIKE AN AMPUTATION . I JUST KNEW SOME PART OF ME WAS MISSING . AND ALONE . UNDER THE SINK . ONE NIGHT . I BORE THE FRUITS OF BLISS UPON THE DISHRAGS OF DESPAIR . JOHN . THRUST THE ROLE OF MOTHER WHEN MY SOUL WAS STILL A LOVER . ALL MY MILK RAN DRY AS ALL MY DREAMS RAN

SOMETHING'S WRONG WITH US . YOU SEE . I DON'T THINK OUR EYES ARE MADE TO SEE THE LIGHT . YOU SEE . NOT ONE OF US BELIEVES WE'LL DIE ALONE . BY DITCH . BY SIDE OF ROAD . ALONE . TONGUE OUT . NOT FOR A LAST DRINK . FOR A LAST KISS . DEAR . JOHN . EYES WIDE OPEN . NOT TO SEE TRUTH . BUT TO SEE YOU . JOHN . DEAR . NOT A ONE OF US BELIEVES WE'LL DIE LIKE DOGS .

WET . FOR ALL I CARED THEY
COULD HAVE CRAWLED AWAY AND
DIED . I THINK ONE DID . CHRIST I
DON'T KNOW . I CAN'T COUNT .
YOU SEE .

101

HOW CAN I KNOW WHAT I KNOW . AND STILL DO WHAT I DO . LOVE YOU .

THAT'S AN INTERESTING
QUESTION . DON'T WORRY IT
HONEY . REST ASSURED
WHEREVER I AM . AND WHATEVER
I SAY . I'M USING YOU . YOU'RE
BEING WORKED SO HARD . HONEY .
YOU SHOULD NEGOTIATE FOR A
FEE .

THE SEED OF OUR SEPARATION GREW AS NATURALLY AS LOVE . IT
STARTED GROWING IN MY STOMACH . I BEGAN TO COMPENSATE FOR
MY UNHAPPINESS WITH FOOD . BUNNY AND I'D SPEND TWENTY
MINUTES GETTING EACH OTHER PAST YONAH SHIMMEL'S KNISHERY .
WITH BUNNY IT WAS TO BE EXPECTED . BUT I'D ALWAYS PRIDED
MYSELF ON WATCHING MY HAUNCH LINE .

IT WAS GROTESQUE . I BLEW UP LIKE A BALLOON . ALONE ONE NIGHT
AND MISERABLE I WORKED ONE TOOTH INTO THE ICEBOX LOCK AND
SPRUNG THE DOOR . I ATE TWO CLUB STEAKS . SALAD NICOISE . HALF
A PLATE OF FETTUCINI CON FUNGI . CREME DE MARRON . SOME WON
TON IN BLACK BEAN SAUCE . A BOARD OF SUSHI . CURRY MURGH
MASSALAM . ONE BOWL OF TANGINE WITH CAMEL BUTTER ON THE
SIDE . TWO TACOS . AND A PIROGI WITH BORSCHT .

102 AFTERWARDS I POURED A BOTTLE OF PERRIER INTO MY WATER DISH AND
LAY THERE WITH MY TONGUE IN IT AND MY EYES CLOSED . THEN I HAD
A DUODENAL ORGASM . TRES PSYCHEDELIQUE .

AS A DOG SITTER BUNNY WAS A GODSEND . I FOUND HIM IN SCREW
UNDER . APARTMENTS TO SHARE . ANIMAL LOVER . I CALLED . I
CALLED . HELP . BUNNY SAID . WHERE ARE YOU . I SAID . IN THE
BAGGAGE ROOM UNDER AN IRISH SETTER . BUNNY SAID . I'LL HOP
RIGHT OVER . HE WAS A GODSEND .

IT'S ALWAYS A LITTLE DIFFICULT TO RECOGNIZE ONE SENT FROM
GOD . BUT I SHOULD HAVE KNOWN . HE STOOD OUT SO . DRESSED
FROM HEAD TO TOE IN RABBIT .
THE FLIGHT HAD BEEN AGONY . MY SHREDDED NEWSPAPER WAS
DRENCHED . BUNNY SAID . YOU MUST BE STARVING . HOW ABOUT
SOME MEXICAN FOOD . I HOWLED . MY HEAD WAS SET ABLAZE WITH
MEMORIES .

COULD I HAVE READ IN MY CARDS THE SIGN OF THE HUNGRY DOG .
JOHN . SO DESPERATE UPON FILLING UP ITS HOLES . EMPTIED OF
LOVE . WITH ANY FARE . I WOULD HAVE RECOGNIZED THE SEED OF
SEPARATION SPROUTING IN MY REFRIED BEANS . BACK AT OUR
PARTING FETE AT LOS BURRITOS CRUSADOS IN SAN PEDRO . BUT I
WAS A DUMB DOG . I THOUGHT IT WAS AN ONION .

AS I POURED MY HEART OUT TO BUNNY YOU POURED BACK INTO ME .
HOW YOU LOOKED IN THE CANDLELIGHT WOLFING DOWN YOUR
ENCHILADA . SNAPPING FOR TWO MARGHARITAS . REMEMBER JOHN

HI . . I'M . . HAVING . . WHAT
MAYBE YOU'D CALL A POWER
FAILURE . WHAT HAPPENS . WELL
LET'S SEE . WHAT HAPPENS .

HOW THE MANAGER CAME AND POINTED TO ME SAYING . CAN'T YOU LOCK HER IN THE CAR . I WAS MORTIFIED . HE BROUGHT UP THE STATE BOARD OF HEALTH . I BROUGHT UP MY GUACOMOLE . THAT BLEW IT . THE MAN SUGGESTED TICO TACO .

YOU FLIPPED HIM THE FINGER . JOHN . I REMEMBER . YOU . SWORD IN HAND . AGAINST THE POWERS . PARTING US . TRAPPING US IN THEIR CONSERVATIVE VIEWS . TELLING US . WE WERE NO GOOD FOR EACH OTHER . BUNNY WAS ALL EARS . I PAINTED YOU AS A WHITE KNIGHT JOHN . THE WAY YOU TOOK OUT MY DOGGIE TRANQS IN THE L.A. INTERNATIONAL AIRPORT . LIKE THEY WERE A POTION IN A SUICIDE PACT . I SAID . NOT ON TOP OF THE MARGARITAS . YOU SAID .

ROSE . YOUR NERVES . YOU WERE RIGHT . I WAS A WRECK . YOU WRAPPED TWO DOGGIE TRANQS IN A FLOUR TORTILLA THAT YOU'D STUFFED IN YOUR POCKET . I GOT THEM DOWN . AND TOOK A LONG DRINK OUT OF THE TOILET BOWL .

IT WAS ALL DOWN FROM THERE . RIGHT INTO THE PASSION PITS . HOW WE PLOTTED . YOU SITTING ON THE HOPPER SEAT . ME PACING UNDERNEATH THE STALLS . WE'D HAVE TO BE CAREFUL . AGREED . WE'D HAVE TO PLAY A SOCIAL GAME . AVOID EACH OTHER AT PARTIES . RENDEZVOUS IN THE PARK . PLOTS AND COUNTERPLOTS . MIDNIGHT WALKINGS . STOLEN KISSES . BETWEEN MY PISSES . THE AURA OF DECEPTION WENT ENTIRELY AGAINST MY GRAIN . WHEN ALL I WANTED WAS TO DOG YOUR FOOTSTEPS IN THE SUNLIGHT . I WANTED TO LICK YOUR ASS . AND BITE YOUR HAND IN THE MOVIES . OH JOHN .

I'D DISH IT UP TO BUNNY OVER AND OVER . OUR DISCUSSIONS WERE ALWAYS OVER DINNER . THESE TENDED TO BE LATE INTIMATE AFFAIRS . HE'D COME BACK FROM HIS LEATHER BAR AT THREE OR FOUR IN THE

WELL . THE LIGHTS GO OFF . AND . MY WHOLE SYSTEM GOES OFF . WHAT . MY SOUND SYSTEM . IT GOES OFF . AND THE STOVE AND THE ICEBOX . THEY GO OFF . WHAT YOU HEAR IS JUST MY PORTABLE . IT'S GOT A FOUR INCH SPEAKER AND A TWO INCH SCREEN . AND NEXT TO WHAT I NEED IT'S NOTHING .

DID I OVERLOAD MY CIRCUIT . WHAT DOES THAT MEAN . WHAT DID I HAVE ON . JUST ABOUT EVERYTHING . YES . UH HUH . YES I HAD MY OVEN ON . WELL I'M COOKING . YEAH . RIGHT NOW I'M COOKING . OH . SOMETHING FOR MY SWEET TOOTH .

UH HUH . CALL ME . ROSE . WELL WHICH DO YOU PREFER . CON OR ED . WELL ED . IS THAT WHAT YOU THINK . YOU THINK I BLEW MY FUSE . DID I LOOK IN MY FUSE BOX . NO . WHY . BECAUSE IT'S NOT A FUSE . IT'S BEEN HAPPENING ALL NIGHT . USUALLY IT COMES RIGHT BACK ON . I THINK IT'S MY POWER . NO . NO JUST TAKE IT FROM ME . IT'S THE POWER .

104 BUNNY AND I BECAME LOVERS . JOHN . DON'T BE JEALOUS .
SEXUALLY WE WERE INCOMPATIBLE . THERE WAS NOTHING BETWEEN
US BUT THE TRUTH . WE BECAME LOVERS OF THE TRUTH . SOUPER
APRES SOUPER WE'D COME ON TO IT . HIDING . UNDER A PARSLEYED
POTATO . OR IN THE HEART OF AN ARTICHOKE . OR THE MARROW OF A
BONE . THEN WE'D TASTE IT . LIKE A CHARMES CHAMBERTIN 1961 .
AND DROWN .

WELL I CAN'T WAIT UNTIL THE
MORNING . I'M WORKING TONIGHT .
WELL I'M WORKING ON A FILM .
WHAT KIND OF A FILM . WELL IT'S
KIND OF A THIN FILM BETWEEN
MYSELF AND SOME EXPERIENCE .

OH YEAH . UH HUH . THEN YOU'RE
A FILM BUFF TOO . OH . EXCUSE
ME . YOU'RE A FILMMAKER . UH
HUH . 8 OR 16 . SUPER 16 . WOW .
SO YOU'RE A SUPER 16 .

ME . I'M MORE OF A CUTTER . BUT
I LIVED WITH A SHOOTER . ONCE .
WHAT DID HE LOOK LIKE . WELL .
KIND OF LIKE A TRACER BULLET .
YEAH . THE KIND THAT SHOOTS OUT
LOOKING FOR A TARGET . BUT THEY
NEVER HIT ANYTHING .

WOULD I LIKE TO SEE YOUR
FOOTAGE . SURE ED . WHEN DO
YOU SHOW IT . YOU'D SET UP A
PRIVATE SHOWING . THAT'S VERY
PROFESSIONAL . YOU'D JUST POP
OUT AND SLAP IT ON MY
PROJECTOR . THAT'S FAR OUT .

BUT ED . ED . ED LISTEN . ED . YOU
CAN'T PROJECT ON ME YET . I
DON'T HAVE MY POWER ON . OF

COURSE I PAID MY BILL . I'M NOT THE TYPE OF PERSON WHO'D FUCK OVER A UTILITY .

WELL YOU KNOW WHERE TO REACH ME . YOU'VE GOT MY BILLING NUMBER . YES I AM A LITTLE LET DOWN . ED . I WAS GETTING ALL WIRED UP .

YOU WOULD . YOU'D TURN ME ON . NOW . IN THE MIDDLE OF THE NIGHT . I JUST BET YOU SAY THAT TO ALL YOUR FELLOW FILMMAKERS . NO . NO . DON'T LISTEN TO ME . I'M JUST ALONE . AND POWERLESS . AND NATURALLY MISTRUSTFUL . YOU KNOW WHAT MY TROUBLE IS . I JUST GOT TO GET CONNECTED .

YOU TURN ME ON ED . YOU WANT TO OPEN UP MY BREAKER BOX . YOU WANT TO SPLICE ME . MAN . YOU GOT A HOT LINE THERE . YOU WANT TO READ MY METER . YOU TURN ME ON ED . I BET WE CAN WORK TOGETHER . YOU LIKE TO ZOOM . BABY . LIP SYNC . YEAH . OH . YOU'RE THE HOUSE OF JUICE . OH YEAH . YOU JIVE MY JUICER .

ONE NIGHT OVER SHISH KEBOB . I LOVE LAMB ON THE SPIT . I TOLD HIM HOW MUCH YOU LOOKED LIKE MY FATHER . I ONLY SAW HIM ONCE . MY MOTHER POINTED HIM OUT TO ME ONE NIGHT IN THE MOONLIGHT . HE WAS EATING CHICKEN . BOY DID HE LOVE CHICKEN . HE WAS SHOT EATING CHICKEN . IT WAS THE FOX IN HIM . DADDY AND I . HAVE A STREAK OF THE FOXY .

BUNNY GRABBED THE BOLSTER AND HE BEAT ME TO A PULP . I BIT HIS EAR AND SWALLOWED HIS EAR RING . NO SHIT . I WAS GETTING OFF . I HAD THIS KIND OF FOXY GRIN ON ONE SIDE OF MY MUZZLE . WHERE HAVE YOU BEEN . ALL MY LIFE . HONEY BUNNY . I HAD THIS FOXY SNARL IN MY THROAT .

AS ALWAYS AT MY FIRST RESPONSE HE HEADED FOR THE PLANTS . HE WAS A PLANT NUT . HAD THEM BROUGHT IN BY THE TRUCK LOAD .

106 THIS TIME I WENT AFTER HIM . FOUND HIM HIDING BY THE CARROT PLANTER . UNDER A FICUS DIVERSAFOLIO . HIS HEAD WAS UP HIS ASS SO FAR HE LOOKED LIKE A FUR COAT FOR A DONUT . I RIPPED INTO HIS RABBIT SUIT . HE POPPED HIS TONGUE OUT . FRENCHED MY EAR . AND CRAWLED UNDER A WANDERING JEW . HE'D TAPED A COTTON TAIL LIGHT ON HIS BUTT . THAT BOY WAS A GOURMET . I CHOMPED . HE SQUEAKED . WE SPLIT . NOT EVEN A GOOD BYE . OH MAN YOU SHOULD HAVE SEEN THE MOTHERFUCKER GO . DOWN THE STAIRS AND OUT THE DOOR AND INTO A VW .

OUTSIDE THERE WAS A FEELING IN THE AIR I COULDN'T PUT MY PAW ON . KEPT SNIFFING FOR IT . NOSE TO THE WIND . AND THEN IT BROKE . LIKE A COLD SWEAT . SNOW .

I DON'T KNOW HOW YOU'LL TAKE THIS JOHN . AS A WARNING OR A THREAT . OR EVEN WORSE . A CURSE . BUT BE ADVISED . I'VE REALIZED . MY LIFE HAS CHANGED . IT'S TAKEN A TRULY INWARD TURN . MY FEELINGS HAVE BECOME THE FACTS . THE DEEPER I FEEL . THE BIGGER THE DEAL . AND OUTSIDE I FELT SO PROFOUND I CONTROLLED THE WEATHER .

SNOW . IT WAS THE REAL THING BABY . THE SKY WAS FULL OF THE SHIT . YOU BETTER BELIEVE IT . I WAS SNOWING .

THE RABBIT WAS WARMING UP ITS ENGINE . WHICH WAS LOGICAL . THE WIND CHILL BEING A MINUS FORTY FOUR . I CREPT UP ON HIS PLAYBOY STICKER . STEP AT A TIME . LAID BACK . EARS DOWN . FUR UP . TONGUE OUT . DROOLING A LITTLE FOR THE FULL EFFECT .

I WISH YOU COULD HAVE SEEN ME JOHN . MY STUFF WAS SPINNING LIKE A SLOT MACHINE . AND COMING UP ALL CHERRIES . I WAS ALL NOSE . A META NOSE . I WAS RIGHT ON THE RABBIT BEAM . I READ ITS SIGNALS . IT WAS BLEEPING FOR A LEFT TURN .

MAN YOU JINGLE GENERATORS ALL OVER TOWN . THEY SAY YOU'VE GOT ATOMIC PILES .

DUMB JOHN .

BUNNY . SONNY . LET ME TELL YOU SOMETHING FUNNY . WE'RE LOCKED IN SYMBIOSIS HONEY . I'M YOUR HOT DOG . YOU'RE MY YUMMY . AND THAT'S WHAT I LIKE ABOUT THE SOUTH .

I COULD SMELL EVERYTHING . THE PAST . THE FUTURE . THE WAY OF
THE WORLD . THE TRAIL OF THE SPIRIT . I COULD SMELL EVERYTHING
BUT A RAT . I WAS AT LAST . ON EARTH . WITH HONOR . I WAS A
PREDATOR . I HAD A FLEETING VISION OF YOU ON YOUR BACK BEFORE
ME . SHOWING ME YOUR BELLY . AS IS CUSTOMARY . TO A MASTER .

BUNNY . SONNY . LET ME TELL YOU
SOMETHING FUNNY . WE'RE LOCKED IN
SYMBIOSIS HONEY . I'M YOUR HOT DOG .
YOU'RE MY YUMMY . AND THAT'S WHAT I LIKE
ABOUT THE SOUTH .

THE RABBIT PEELED A u AND SKIDDED DOWN THE WRONG WAY OF A
ONE WAY STREET . I TRAILED THE TRACKS IN THE FALLING SNOW . IT
WAS EASY . THEY BEING FOUR PLY STEEL BELTED RADIALS . IT WAS
PLAIN OBVIOUS . THAT RABBIT WAS MAKING FOR THE PARK .

IN THE PARK I SAW THE LIGHTS OF HELL . THEY WERE BALLS OF
GREEN AND BALLS OF SALMON . THEY FLEW RIGHT AT ME . I WAS
REALLY UP . MAN . I WAS HIGH AS A LAMP POST . I SAW THE RABBIT
ZIG AND ZAG . THAT DUDE WAS RUNNING A SLALOM AROUND THE
TEETER TOTTERS . THEN I HEARD A CRASH . IT WAS A SOFT CRASH .
KIND OF A WHEEZE . LIKE WHEN YOU SQUEEZE . THE AIR OUT OF AN
ACCORDIAN . THAT POOR CRITTER HAD FOLDED UP AGAINST THE
MONKEY BARS . KIND OF A PLEATED EFFECT . THE DOOR WAS OPEN
AND THE HORN WAS STUCK . THE SOUND WAS HIGH AND LONELY AND
IT HIT A FLATTED FIFTH OVER THE WIND .

I SQUINTED . ALL AROUND ME RAGED THE BLIZZARD OF THE SEASON .
YOU KNOW . THE ONE THAT NEVER MADE THE PAPERS . FORTY TWO
INCHES OF PURE DRIVEN WILL POWER . THE POWDERY KIND . THERE
WERE UP DRAFTS . DOWN FALLS . SNOW SPOUTS . ICE BALLS . ALL
MANNER OF THE BAROQUE . NO JOKE . SAW A COUPLE OF THOSE
LITTLE WHIRLIGIG TORNADOES ROUNDING SECOND AND HEADING FOR
HOME ON THE SOFT BALL FIELD .

108 HOT DAMN . THERE WENT THE RABBIT UP THE HILL . LOOKED LIKE A
SQUIRREL IN SNOWSHOES . KIND OF SWISHY . NO HE WASN'T GOING .
HE WAS COMING . NOPE HE WAS GOING . NOPE HERE HE COMES .
NOPE . THERE HE GOES . BACK TRACKS . SIDETRACKS . RETRACTS .
HERE WAS THE GRAPHICS OF HESITATION . THE HEAD OF ONE INSTINCT
IN THE JAWS OF ANOTHER . BUNNY WANTS IT . NO HE DOESN'T . SURE
HE DOES . THAT BUNNY WANTS THE BUSINESS . SEE . I HAD THE
RABBIT DEAD TO RIGHTS .

I'M SURE YOU GET THE PICTURE JOHN . ALL THIS WAS QUITE
OBSESSIVE . JUST LIKE EVERYTHING I DO . LIKE LOVING YOU . JUST
ANOTHER LITTLE SHOWCASE FOR MY CREATIVE URGE CALLED **LOVE WAS
KILLING ME AND HERE I WAS KILLING HIM AND LOVING IT** . WHAT A DUMB MESS . I
COULD ALWAYS COUNT ON BUNNY TO GO AND MAKE A DUMB MESS OF
MY PORTRAIT . GOD DAMN IT . HERE HE WAS AT IT AGAIN . AS MY
SHADOW BLED ACROSS THE SNOW AND LAY UPON ITS COLD
CONFIGURATIONS LIKE A DOOMSDAY MAP . ALL MANNER OF THE
GOTHIC . WHAT DO YOU KNOW . A GAP APPEARED . AND THERE I WAS
ON THE OUTSKIRTS OF LAS VEGAS .

LET ME EXPLAIN . NOW IN THE LIVES OF ANIMALS THERE COME
THESE TIMES OF SYNCHRONOUS PROJECTIONS . I SAID SYNCHRONOUS
PROJECTIONS . TIMES WHEN THEIR LITTLE OVER HEATED HEARTS ARE
RIGHT IN PHASE WHILE THEIR LITTLE SNOW BALL MINDS ARE MILES
AWAY . YOU KNOW WHAT THAT IS . IT'S THAT OLD .

I LOOK AT YOU AND I SEE ME . AND YOU LOOK
AT ME AND YOU SEE YOU . IT'S DO SEE DO
AND DOO WAKA DOO AND THAT'S WHAT I LIKE
ABOUT THE SOUTH .

THIS IS THE MECHANISM OF ATTACHMENT . IT TAKES A CERTAIN
COMMITMENT TO STUPIDITY . BUT THAT'S NEVER A PROBLEM .
CONFIDENTIALLY I THINK IT'S THE TAP ROOT OF LOVE .

THERE . FROM OUT OF MY FOXY LAIR . PEERED I . WITH AN UNBELIEVING STARE . AND PERCEIVED A HARE . ON THE OUTSKIRTS OF LAS VEGAS .

THERE I WAS . IN BUNNY'S POINT OF VIEW . THE RABBIT KNEW . IT WAS ALL OVER BETWEEN US BUT THE TWITCHING . AND HIS FEELINGS AS REGARDS OUR SAD AFFAIR WERE MORE PROFOUND THAN MINE . SO I . WAS HIS . JOHN . I WAS HIS . THERE ON THE OUTSKIRTS OF LAS VEGAS . BECAUSE AFTER ALL IS SAID AND DONE . BUNNY WAS A COWBOY . I WAS HIS LIKE YOU'LL BE MINE . JOHN . AFTER ALL THIS HIT AND RUN . IT'S STILL ME . BABY . I'M STILL A DOG .

IT WAS A HUNDRED AND SEVEN AT SIX A.M. I BIT HIS HEAD OFF AND STUCK IT IN A GOPHER HOLE . BOY WAS I MAD . AND STUMBLED THROUGH THE TUMBLEWEED TO SECOND AVENUE AND FISHED AN OLD BAGEL OUT OF A GARBAGE CAN . AND CRAWLED HOME UNDER THE SINK . AND BROUGHT UP THE BAGEL . I WAS SO MAD . I HAD PUPPIES .

THIS WAS THE GOD DAMN FUCKING LIMIT . JOHN . I MEAN IT WAS GROSS . LIFE . DUMPED IN MY LAP . WHEN ALL I ASKED FOR WAS A LITTLE POETRY . I PICKED UP THE PHONE TO CALL YOU . IT WAS ON VACATION DISCONNECT . WELL WHAT COULD I HAVE SAID TO YOU . CONGRATULATIONS .

I GREW SNAPPY AND METAPHORICAL . BROADWAY DROPPED BY . HE SNUCK IN DOWNSTAIRS WITH THE POSTMAN AND CHEWED AT MY

THE DOG CONTEMPLATES THE QUESTION . WHO'S IN WHO'S SCENARIO .

WHOEVER'S IN DEEPER .

ROSE READS WHO'S WHO'S . IN THE ANIMAL WORLD .

CLEARLY I HAD BEEN MISTREATED . AND NOW . I WANTED SOME RESPECT . I SEE THIS . NOW . IN RETROSPECT . I SEE THE WHOLE MOVEMENT . IN MY LIFE . AWAY FROM MY BASIC ANIMAL NATURE .

WHILE THE LITTER NAPPED IN MY ARMPITS . AND SNEEZED IN MY EAR . I DEVELOPED AN ESCAPIST PERSONALITY . I DREAMED . AND REMEMBERED . AND LISTENED TO WHN TEN FIFTY . AND AVOIDED MIRRORS . PETRIFIED THAT I'D AGED .

110 DOOR . I SAID . SHOVE OFF . MAN . YOU'LL FUCK UP MY WELFARE .
HE STARTED TO CRY . I SAID . IT'S OVER . MAN . I'M JUST SOME
BITCH YOU KNOCKED UP IN THE PARK . WHO NEEDS YOU .

HE WAS THERE FOR DAYS . CHEWING UP THE BASEBOARD . THAT
DUMB FUCK WAS IN LOVE WITH ME . WHAT A DUMB FUCK . I
THOUGHT . IN MY OBJECTIVITY .

I SHOCKED MYSELF . I BROKE HIS HEART . HE STARTED PINING
'ROUND THE MIDNIGHT SUPERETTE . LAPPING UP THE BROKEN
RIPPLE . WHEN HE GOT INTO BOONE'S FARM GOLDEN APPLE I KNEW
HE WAS A GONER .

NOW WHAT DID I HAVE AGAINST THAT POOR DUDE . THAT HE WAS A
DOG . I GUESS . I WAS A BITCH BY NATURE . BUT CLEARLY NOT . BY
TEMPERAMENT . BY TEMPERAMENT I WOULD ALWAYS BE
VOLUPTUOUS . IN THE PRIVACY OF MY DEN . A CONVERTED LINEN
CLOSET UNDER THE STEREO . I GATHERED STRENGTH FOR A SECOND
GREAT ASSAULT ON YOUR AFFECTIONS .

THERE WAS FOOD IN THE HOUSE . THANKS TO BUNNY . AND A GOOD
RECIPE FOR LAPIN AU CHASSEUR . I ATE PERFUNCTORILY . KEEPING A
FOOT FOR LUCK . AND POPPED A PET CAL . BUT MY HEART FASTED
FOR FORTY DAYS . I'D ABIDE . BUT NOW I HAD TO MAKE A LIVING .

LOVE WAS IMPOSSIBLE .
FANTASIES ENCROACHED . IN MY
FANTASIES I CALCULATED AND
MANIPULATED AND WON VICTORIES
AND DISDAINED THEM . IT WAS
INEVITABLE .

I ENTERED THE ART WORLD .

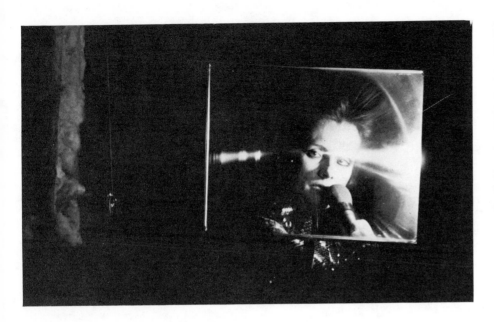

MY ENTRY INTO THE ART WORLD WAS INAUSPICIOUS AT FIRST . YOU KNOW HOW IT GOES . HANGING OUT . HANGING IN . HANGING AROUND . I TOOK A COURSE AT K9 COMMANDO PATROL IN YONKERS AND GOT A JOB ON THE DOOR AT O.K. HARRIS .

YOU KNOW WHAT MADE IT EASY JOHN . THE MOVEMENT . DOGS WERE MOVING . MAN RAY HAD HAD A SPREAD IN **AVALANCHE** . GLAZA CAME OUT WITH **MY LIFE ON THE FLOOR** . I WENT TO OPENINGS . I WAS IN A POSITION TO HEAR A LOT OF GOSSIP . IT WAS A GOOD DECISION . UNDER THE TABLE . I LEARNED THE TRICKS OF THE TRADE . THEY WEREN'T HARD . I LEARNED TO SHAKE HANDS . PLAY DEAD . AND BEG . TWO WEEKS LATER I PICKED UP A CAPS GRANT .

WHAT I DESCRIBE . LOVE . IS A CHANGE OF GEARS . A BACK SHIFT INTO ANOTHER COGWHEEL OF BEHAVIOR . BOURGEOIS BEHAVIOR . LOVE GROUND DOWN TO LOW . TO NEUTRAL . TO REVERSE .

I WAS DEVOURED BY MY LOVE . MY LOVE WAS DEVOURED BY EXIGENCIES . THE PUPPY DOO PILED UP IN CORNERS . THE FLEAS IN DRAWERS . I LONGED FOR HELP . IN THE HOUSE . BUNNY I CALLED . BUT MY BUNNY WAS DEVOURED TOO .

NOW . SEE YOURSELF AS A HEAVYWEIGHT . WEIGHT TWO HUNDRED TWELVE . HEIGHT SIX . THREE . REACH EIGHTY . CHEST NORMAL . FORTY THREE . CHEST EXPANDED . FORTY FIVE . FOREARM . THIRTEEN AND ONE HALF . WAIST . THIRTY FOUR . THIGH . TWENTY SIX . CALF . SEVENTEEN . NECK . SEVENTEEN AND ONE HALF . WRIST . EIGHT . ANKLE . NINE AND ONE HALF . FIST . THIRTEEN .

112 JDR III CALLED . COULD I USE HIS FROZEN FUNDS UP IN ALASKA . A COMMISSION . ART PARK WANTED A DOG RUN . SIGNED . THEN CAME MY ENTREE INTO EXXON . DOG POWER FOR SMALLER VEHICLES . THIS PLAYED HAVOC WITH THE PRICE OF OIL . THERE WERE MIDDLE EASTERN REVERBERATIONS . MARION JAVITS TOOK ME FOR KALKAN TARTAR . THE HUNT FOUNDATION TRIED TO BUY ME OFF WITH BLUE CHIP CATSUP . I WAS INVITED TO SPEAK AT THE ANNUAL SAINT MIDAS DAY CONFERENCE ON ART FUNDING AT THE FELT FORUM . I WAS THE MAIN EVENT .

SPEAKING PUBLICLY I PICKED UP A BARK WORSE THAN MY BITE . THIS WAS PARTICULARLY USEFUL IN THE POLITICAL ARENA . I COULD SNAP AND YAP AND SNARL WITHOUT THREATENING A SOUL . THERE WAS ONLY ONE TRICK I HAD TROUBLE WITH . KEEPING MY NOSE CLEAN . KEEP YOUR NOSE CLEAN . ROSE . ALL MY FRIENDS WOULD ADVISE . I COULDN'T DO IT . EVERY TIME I SNIFFED AN ASSHOLE I GOT A NEW IDEA . I WENT INTO A TRANCE . I COULDN'T KEEP MY NOSE CLEAN BECAUSE . BY IMPLICATION . IT TOUCHED THE HEART OF MY CREATIVE PROCESS .

IT WAS ABOUT THAT TIME THAT LOIS LUNCH INCORPORATED GOT HOLD OF ME . SHE GOT HOLD OF ME BY TICKLING MY EARS . WHICH ALWAYS MAKES ME CLOSE MY EYES . WHEN I OPENED MY EYES I WAS ON A SNAKESKIN LEASH AT MADISON AND 38TH . DEEP IN THE HEART OF CURB YOUR DOG COUNTRY .

LOIS SAID . CARE FOR A DRINK . SHE POURED ME A TAB INTO AN ABANDONED HUB CAP . ICE . SHE TOED IN SOME SLUSH . WE SHOULD COUNT THOSE CALORIES TILL YOUR PROFILE'S IN PEOPLE . I SAID . I'M NOT PEOPLE MATERIAL . SHE SAID . RIGHT . FIELD AND STREAM .

THE RIGHT HAND WRAPPED IN NUMBER 4450 HERRING BONE TAPE . LIST . TWO FIFTY . WEARING A NUMBER 2106 TOP PRO SAFETY GUARD SIX OUNCE FIGHTING GLOVE . LIST . SIXTY NINE NINETY FIVE . DRIPPING NOSE BLOOD . THE LEFT HAND FLOURISHING A FIST ALOFT . BROW FURROWED . EYE SLIT . LIP CURLED . SHOWING A NUMBER 4404 EVERGUARD DOUBLE WHITE PARA RUBBER MOUTH PIECE . DANCING . CROWN OF SWEAT . HEEL FLUNG AND KNEE UPLIFTED . UPON YOUR VERY OWN FLESHY HEAP . DOWN FOR THE COUNT . FLAMES OF RIGHT KNOWLEDGE . FORMING A HALO . OVER YOUR 4011 TOP PRO HEAD GUARD . WITH CHEEK PROTECTOR .

LET US PRAY . ROSE . A FILMMAKER'S PRAYER .

VOUCHSAFE ME THE POWER TO FUCK ART . AND SETTLE DOWN . IN THE WORLD . OF ENTERTAINMENT . SELF ENTERTAINMENT . TEACHERS

MS. INC. I SAID . I HATE TO SAY THIS BUT I'M NOT AN AMBITIOUS
SORT OF BREED . I'M A MOTHER FIRST . SHE SAID . WHERE DO YOU
WANT TO BE THREE YEARS FROM NOW . I SAID . I JUST WANT TO MAKE
A LIVING FOR MYSELF AND MY DEPENDENTS . HOW MANY . SHE SAID .
NINE . I SAID . TOPANGA CANYON . SHE SAID . THREE YEARS FROM
NOW YOU COULD BE UP IN TOPANGA CANYON . YOU'RE A DOG . DEAR .
THAT'S HAVING ITS DAY . AND NOW'S THE TIME TO TALK CAREER
PLANNING .

MS. INC. I SAID . I HATE TO SAY THIS . BUT IF I HAD MY CHOICE I
WOULDN'T LIVE UNDER A ROOF AT ALL . A COZY DEN OF THE TUNDRA .
NORTH IN SUMMER TO FOLLOW THE CARIBOU . I'D WATCH MY DIET .
FIELD MICE AND LICHEN . THE TROUBLE IS YOU JUST CAN'T FIND THAT
SORT OF THING AT A COMMUTING DISTANCE FROM NEW YORK . LOIS
SAID . ROSE . MY DEAR . YOU'RE JUST AN ANIMAL LIKE ANY OTHER
ANIMAL . YOU'RE AN UNDERDEVELOPED SPECIES IN A LAND OF
OPPORTUNITY . YOU WANT IT ALL . YOU WANT IT NOW . YOU ARE A
WEST SIDE STORY . YOU'RE A NATIVE SON . YOU'RE AN AMERICAN
TRAGEDY BABY . YOU'RE WHAT MAKES SAMMY RUN . I KNOW YOU .
SCHLEPPED HERE FROM SOME DARK CONTINENT . SOME MOUNTAIN
TOP . SOME FUCKED UP ART DEPARTMENT IN WISCONSIN . A RURAL
ANIMAL . HISTORY OF PERSECUTION . OFF TO THE INNER CITY . GET
YOUR STREET SMARTS . INTO CRIME . DO TIME . THE SYSTEM ELUDES
YOU . TO FIND A WAY IN . YOU ENTER THE FIGHT GAME . YOU START
BOXIN' . AN ALL FRONTS ASSAULT ON THE DIVISIONS . LIGHTWEIGHTS .
WELTERS . THE HEAVIES . AND THEN THE CLASSES . FROM THE
PINNACLE OF THE HEAVYWEIGHT DIVISION YOU BITE INTO THE MIDDLE
CLASSES . INTO . AND FROM THERE INTO ELECTIVE OFFICE . YOU MEET
AT SUMMITS . WRITE HISTORY . RACE TO SPACE THEN A QUADRUPEDAL
FATIGUE SETS IN . YOU LEAN TO CONSERVATIVE INVESTMENTS .
BECOME A CLOSET DECADENT . A GOURMET . IN A FIT OF ENNUI YOU
THROW YOURSELF UNDER A GOLF CART .

114 THAT'S HOW IT IS . EVERYWHERE . EXCEPT IN TOPANGA CANYON . SHE
TOOK OUT A CONTRACT . LOIS . I SAID . FUCK OFF . I'VE ALREADY
SIGNED WITH WILLIAM MORRIS .

OF THE FAITH . ROBERT . GEORGE .
AND FRANCIS FORD . AND YOU TOO
STANLEY . GIVE ME EACH DAY .
THE DAILY BREAD . TO FASCINATE
MYSELF FOREVER .
MAKETH ME TO LIE DOWN . IN THE
LIGHT . AND SLEEP RIGHT THROUGH
IT . AND WAKE UP IN THE
DARKNESS . IN TIME TO BUY
POPCORN . YEA THOUGH I WALK
THROUGH THE VALLEY . OF THE
SHADOW . MAY SAG WALK BESIDE
ME . AND GUIDE ME . TO THE
VALLEY OF THE DOLLS . LEAD ME
NOT INTO AESTHETICS . AND
DELIVER ME . FROM SIMPLICITY .
FOR THINE . IS THE DOGDOM . I
MEAN DUMB . AND THE POWER
AND GLORY . OF FISCAL
GRATIFICATION . WHEREIN I SEE .
THE PLASTIC . OF THE REEL .
UNLESS IT'S ALUMINUM . OH
MAN .

I WAS FACED WITH A CRISIS . I'D COLLECTED FIVE COMMISSIONS .
FOUR MATCHING GRANTS . THREE BANK LOANS . TWO FEATURE
SPREADS . AND A PATRON IN A PEAR TREE . I HAD TO DO SOMETHING .
OR ELSE I'D BE SUED . ON THE OTHER HAND . IF I DID . I COULD BLOW
AN INCOME FOR LIFE .

116 SO I MADE MY MOVE . I MOVED OUT OF POLITICS . AND THEN I MOVED DOWN WEST BROADWAY TO SPRING . ACROSS TO GREEN . AND BACK UP TO HOUSTON . I NEUTRALIZED THE PLACE . WHEREVER SOMEONE HAD SHOT THEIR LOAD . I PISSED ON IT . THEN I FOUND SOME RAW SPACE WITH GOOD LIGHT AND A NINE INCH CURB . IT WAS CLEAN . NOT A DOG HAD DUMPED IN A WEEK AND A HALF . IT WAS A NO LOADING ZONE . I PAINTED THE FIREPLUG AND APPLIED FOR A PERMIT TO BUILD A TAX SHELTER .

FORD CALLED . CONGRATULATIONS . WE HEAR YOU'RE INTO REAL ESTATE . THEY ASKED IF I'D BEEN PAINTING LATELY . I MENTIONED MY FIREPLUG . THEY GOT TOUCHY . THEY HADN'T GOT A PRESS RELEASE . WHEN WOULD I OPEN IT .

I DECIDED TO OPEN MY FIREPLUG AT FIVE FORTY FIVE ON SUNDAY MORNING AND CLOSE IT BY SIX FIFTEEN . THAT WAY IT COULD BE DOCUMENTED BEFORE IT WAS NOTICED . THIS WAS A MISTAKE . I FLOODED THE FIRST FLOOR OF ART IN AMERICA .

ART IN AMERICA CAME DOWN ON ME HARD . ROSE IS SIMPLY NOT A CREATIVE INDIVIDUAL . BELIEVE ME THAT HURT . ROSE IS A RIPOFF . SHE'S A MISPELLED DUCHAMP . AND THAT FIREPLUG ISN'T A FIREPLUG EITHER . IT'S AN OLD OLDENBURG .

I WAS OUT OF MY DEPTH . I CLOSED MY EYES AND LET THE SUCKERS HAVE AT ME . I COULD FEEL YOU THERE JOHN . HAVING AT ME . ON TEAT NUMBER THREE . I COULD FEEL ART IN AMERICA ON TEAT NUMBER SEVEN . AFTER THE MILK WAS GONE THERE WAS ALWAYS MY BLOOD . I FELT LIKE A SAINT . LIKE A LEAF IN THE WIND . THERE I WAS . GIVING THE WORLD WHAT IT WANTED . A CORROBORATION OF ITS POWER IN THE FLUTTER OF MY HEART . I DRIFTED OFF . UP TWO POINTS ON THE KARMIC SCALE . STEADY ON THE RICHTER . AND DOWN A QUARTER ON DOW JONES .

NEXT MORNING I HERDED THE LITTER DOWN TO THE PARK AND DUMPED
THEM IN THE DOG RUN . THEN I CUT OUT FOR THE ARBORETUM TO
CHASE SQUIRRELS . I HAD TO BE ALONE .

AS OPPOSED TO RABBITS . SQUIRRELS WERE ESOTERIC FARE . I NEVER
COULD CATCH ONE . IT WAS LIKE CHASING A DREAM . CROUCHED IN
THE SHADOWS OF FLOWERS . WATCHING THE SHADOWS OF BRANCH . I
COULD FEEL A CENTERING . MY MIND WAS LOOKING AT ITSELF .

THE RAG WAS RIGHT . I WAS NOT A CREATIVE INDIVIDUAL . I HAD NO
EYE FOR SPACE AT ALL . HOW COULD I . I HAD MONOSCOPIC VISION .
ONE EYE ON EACH SIDE . I HAD NO DEPTH PERCEPTION . FACE REALITY
ROSE . I SAID . YOU HAVE NO DEPTH . YOU ARE DOOMED TO SEE ONLY
THE SURFACE . THUS I RUMINATED . MUZZLE TO THE EARTH . WHEN
LO . OFF THE WAVING BLADES OF GRASS . ROSE A HAUNTING OF
ODORS . A BOUQUET OF REMORSE . AND OF LOVE UNREQUITTED .
DRIFTING AND ROCKING LIKE UNTO THE SEA . A SMELL . NOT OF
BODIES . BUT OF SOULS .

I INHALED THE ODOR OF PASSIONATE SOULS . ANIMAL PASSIONS .
EBBING AND FLOWING . LIKE TIDES IN THE THRALL OF THE MOON . I
CURLED INTO A BALL AND WAS SET HIGH ADRIFT . LIKE AN INNER
TUBE . SPLAT . ON THE OCEAN OF LOVE . ALL MY AMOURS WASHED
OVER MY BODY . MY SISTERS AND BROTHERS ALL NESTLED MY HEAD .
I SMELLED MY POOR FATHER EATING HIS CHICKEN . TEARS FLOODED
MY EYES . AND THERE WAS MY MOTHER . OH MOTHER . I CRIED . AND
FATHER . I WEPT . AND A SIGH WELLED UP . LIKE A WATERSPOUT . AND
THE SIGH RESOLVED ITSELF INTO A CHORD . AND THE CHORD WAS
MINOR SEVENTH WITH A SUSPENDED FIFTH . AND A VOICE SPAKE . AND
IT SAID UNTO ME .

118 ROSE . THE RAG WAS RIGHT . ROSE YOU ARE NOT A CREATIVE INDIVIDUAL . ALL YOU CAN SEE IS THE SURFACE OF THINGS . YOU HAVE NO DEPTH . BUT LO . BABY . YOU'VE GOT TIME . YOU ARE . THREE . DIMENSIONAL . TOO . YOUR DIMENSIONS . ROSE . ARE ONE TWO AND FOUR .
AND I SPOKE TO THE VOICE . YOU SHUCK ME . VOICE . AND THE VOICE SAID . NO . LO . TIME IS ON YOUR SIDE . YES IT IS . YOU CAN BRING BACK THE PAST . YOU ARE A RECREATIVE . INDIVIDUAL . AND I CALLED OUT . VOICE . THAT BLOWS IT FOR THE ART WORLD DOESN'T IT . AND THE VOICE SAID . YOU'RE ALL SHOW BIZ HONEY .

THAT NIGHT I WENT TO WORK ON THE APARTMENT . I WAS MANIC . BY A TRIUMPH OF WILL . IN A COUP DE THEATRE . I WOULD RECREATE MY HAPPINESS . I WOULD SMELL YOU . BACK . TO ME .

I COVERED THE FLOOR IN A FIGURE EIGHT . THEN CRISS CROSSED IT IN A GRID . NOTHING . OLD TECHNIQUES WERE USELESS . BUT YOU WERE THERE . I KNEW YOU WERE THERE . I KNOCKED OVER THE KITCHEN GARBAGE . AND PROPPED IT UPSIDE DOWN BEFORE A MIDNIGHT WINDOW . AND THERE ON MY HAUNCHES . ON MY CAN . I MEDITATED IN THE LIGHTHOUSE OF THE MOON .

A SIREN ECHOED ACROSS THE STARS . I RAISED MY HEAD AND PUCKERED . BREATHING IN THROUGH MY NOSE . I WAS HOPING TO HIT AN OCTAVE AND A HALF OVER THE AMBULANCE . A HOWL OR TWO ALWAYS CLEARED MY HEAD . BUT I NEVER UTTERED A SOUND . MY MIND EXPLODED WITH A ROSY LIGHT . I SMELLED SOMETHING .

YOU . NO WONDER I COULDN'T FIND YOU IN THE RUG . YOU HAD LEFT THE GROUND . YOU WERE IN THE VERY AIR I BREATHED . THERE . THEN . WAS OUR LIFE . CLINGING LIKE SMOKE TO THE CEILING BEAMS AND WISPING THROUGH THE LEAKS OF LIGHT AROUND THE DOOR . I FOUND THE POPCORN AND THE BUTTER DRIPS BACK BEHIND BUNNY'S

PILE OF GOURMET MAGAZINES . I FOUND MY BLOW JOB IN A KITCHEN
DRAWER BETWEEN THE SARAN WRAP AND AN EXTRA ROLL OF TOILET
PAPER . AND THE NIGHT I DANCED FOR YOU . SOMEHOW THE WHOLE
THING HAD OSMOSED ITSELF INTO THE DIETETIC MAYONNAISE .

I WENT OVER THE RUG LIKE A VACUUM CLEANER . SWITCHED
ATTACHMENTS . AND WENT OVER THE UPHOLSTERY . IT WAS ALL
HERE . SO ARTFULLY ABSTRACTED . SO ART FULL . SO ABSTRACTED .
THE SCENT OF YOUR BOMBER JACKET DRAPED ON A PRESTO LOG . IN A
FIELD OF LEFTOVER RAVIOLI . COURTESY RAUSCHENBERG . THE
COMPLETE PHOENIX STOPOVER . I MUST HAVE BROUGHT THAT WITH
ME . IT MUST HAVE CLUNG TO MY FUR . COMPLETE . WITH LESS THAN
FIVE PER CENT HUMIDITY . THERE IT WAS IN THE BATHROOM
STRETCHED OUT UNDER THE SUN LAMP . COURTESY . GEORGIA
O'KEEFFE . I SNUFFED AND SNORTED RIGHT UP THE WINDOW DRAPES .
AND IN A FLIGHT OF FANCY . FLOATED HIGH ACROSS THE CEILING
BEAMS . HERE WAS A SUBTLETY OF BOUQUET . THE SUBTLETY OF
WHICH ELUDED ME . I BARELY GOT A WIFF OF IT . PERHAPS MY
SEPTUM COULD BE EDUCATED LIKE A PALATE . I LOOKED AHEAD TO
YEARS OF DRUDGERY . NOSE TO THE GRINDSTONE . PERFECTING A
TECHNIQUE . CLASSES . TUITIONS . AND APPRENTICESHIP TO
SOMEBODY BIG IN THE FIELD . AN ELEPHANT OF ART .

SUCH NEW SPACE . SO MANY QUESTIONS . WAS THERE A LITERATURE
ON THE SUBJECT . WHAT WAS THE SUBJECT . OLFACTORY
STEREOPTICS . NO . RESEARCHES IN TEMPS PERDU . NO . PROJECT
DEVELOPMENT FOR INDEPENDENT FILM PRODUCTION . NO . MANIC
STATES IN THE RECREATIVE CONSCIOUSNESS . NO . DOGS . NO . YOU .
NO . ME . NO . ME . IS THERE A LITERATURE ON THE SUBJECT OF . NO
ME . SURE AS SHIT .

120 NOSE IN YOUR DIRTY LAUNDRY . I WAS SNIFFING OUT A TOSUN BAYRAK . WHEN THE THOUGHT OCCURRED TO ME THAT HERE INDEED WAS A SORRY STATE . WHY WAS I SMELLING EVERTHING IN TERMS OF SOMEONE ELSE . HAD ART RIPPED OFF MY MEMORY . WAS OUR LOVE . JOHN . NOT A MOVIE AFTER ALL . BUT A GODDAMN GROUP RETROSPECTIVE . WAS I A DOG . OR A COPYCAT .

I COVERED MY NOSE WITH MY PAW AND VOWED NEVER TO INHALE AGAIN . WHEN . SUDDENLY . THERE YOU WERE . YOU WERE BACK ON THE SCENE AGAIN . I HEARD YOUR THEME MUSIC . BACK IN THE SADDLE AGAIN . I WAS CONFUSED . WHEN HAD I SHOT THIS ENTRANCE . DON'T TELL ME I'D FORGOTTEN . PERHAPS WHEN I WAS YOUNG AND SLIPSHOD . BEFORE I'D LEARNED TO NOTE MY TAKES . NO . IMPOSSIBLE . I NEVER LOSE MY FOOTAGE .

SLOWLY . SO SLOWLY . SO PAINFULLY . IN THE FEVER OF MY WORK AT YOU . MY RECREATIVE WORK . IT COMES TO ME . THAT THIS . IS HERE . THAT THIS . IS NOW . THAT THIS . IS BRAND NEW MATERIAL . HOW WOULD I HANDLE IT .

I STAND HERE BEFORE YOU . PANTING AND SWALLOWING . IN THE CHAOS OF MY MEMORY . AND ONE BY ONE . THE MEMBERS OF MY FAMILY . WAGGING THEIR TAILS . EACH TIPTOE TO ME . AND STAND QUIETLY AROUND ME IN A RING .

HERE WITHIN . THE AURA OF OLD PASSION . FRESHLY REBORN . FRESH TO BE TAKEN . AFRESH BY YOU . HERE DIRECTED . BY THE WISDOM OF THE HEART . THAT DUMBNESS . SO DEEP SEEDED . HERE WE PANT . AND WE SWALLOW . AND LOVE YOU ANEW .

AND WITH QUIVER OF NOSES AND THRASHING OF TAILS . WITH THE
SQUEALS AND EXCESSES OF OUR KIND . WE SHRED THE REMAINS OF
THIS PURGATORY LIKE AN INCRIMINATING DOCUMENT OF OUR PAIN .

WE RIP AND CLAW THE AIR LIKE PILLOWS . THE PILLOWS LIKE THE
AIR . LIKE HOLY IDIOTS . THEIR CLACKERS . FETISHES . AND BELLS .
WE TIE TO OUR PAWS THE TIPS OF OUR TAILS . STRINGS OF SHIT AND
DROOL AND URINE . FESTOONED WITH BANNERS OF THE LAUNDRY BIN .
GARLANDS OF SHAVING CREAM AND CALADRIL . QUALUDE . ARM AND
HAMMER BAKING SODA . FRANKINCENSE . AND MYRRH . LIKE
TERMITES IN A RELIC OF THE CROSS DO WE DEVOUR . IN PAROXYSM
SAINT VITUS DO WE DANCE . LOOSING RIVERS OF ROACHES . HURLING
ROCKETS OF FLEAS . AND CLASHING THE DISHES LIKE GONGS . TILL WE
CAUTERIZE OUR LONGING . WITH THE SWORD OF YOUR RETURN . AND
MAKE OF OUR LOVE NEST . A CESSPOOL OF DEVOTION .

HERE IT IS . JOHN GREED . ALL HANGING OUT . MY GARBAGE PIT OF
LOVE FOR YOU . HERE'S YOUR TEMPLE .

AND WHEN WE . ALCHEMICALLY . TRANSFORM MOLD INTO FILAGREE .
DROPPINGS TO JEWELS . WE ROLL OVER ONTO OUR BACKS . AND MAKE
OBEISANCE . MASTER . PAWING THE AIR . FOR THE CARESS . THE PAT
OF OUR DELIVERANCE .

LESLIE WENT FOR THE KITCHEN MOP TO BEAT THE LIVING SHIT OUT OF
MY BODY . YOU STAYED HER HAND . STAY YOUR HAND . WOMAN . YOU
SPAKE . SHE'S IN A SPECIAL PLACE . SHE'S OUT OF HER MIND .

YOU CARRIED ME TO THE KITCHEN . AND FED ME ALPO OUT OF A CAN . A MAT WAS PROVIDED FOR ME . HOSPITAL WHITE . AND A STRING OF BEADS TO PLAY WITH . WHICH I TRIED TO COUNT . BUT COULDN'T . I SAID . JOHN . YOU SAID . YES ROSE . I SAID . IT'S THE NIGHTTIME . DON'T FORGET TO PRAY FOR ME . I'M LEAVING THE ART WORLD .

PUPPIES . HALF SALUKI . FULLY WEANED MAKE OFFER .

THIS WAS SLAVERY . THIS WAS MY FLESH AND BLOOD . THIS WAS UNCONSTITUTIONAL . I STOOD LIKE A STONE AND I WEPT NOT A TEAR . DO YOU KNOW WHY . JOHN . DEAR .

BECAUSE I WAS TURNED OFF . TO THE SOCIAL ISSUE . I WAS BORED . I SAW ANOTHER ISSUE . I SAW THE LOVE ISSUE .

CHILDREN CAME WITH SHOE BOX BEDS AND DOLLARS CONNED FROM DADDIES . LITTLE BREAST EMPTY MOTHERS . WEE BALL SCRATCHING LOVERS . I SAW MY LITTER FALL IN LOVE . BY CUPID GLANCE . BY LOWERED EYE . FIRST LICKS . FIRST TEARS . FIRST SCRATCHINGS OF THE EARS . BY NIP . BY STROKE . BY DRAMA OF AMBIVALENCE . BY PRAYER FOR DELIVERANCE . I SAW THE BUD OF ATTACHMENT FLOWER . SO UNLIKE A LOTUS . SO EXACTLY LIKE A ROSE . HERE WERE THE TERMS OF MY ENLIGHTENMENT . I WAS THE MANY PETALED VERSION OF THE WRONG FUCKING FLOWER .

OUR LAST COMMUNICATION . JOHN . I FLASH BACK TO OUR LAST COMMUNICATION . IT ORNAMENTS MY MIND LIKE A TATTOO . BLUE GREEN . AND INDELIBLE OVER MEMORY'S TISSUE OF SCARS .

IT WAS A SIMPLE MORNING PROMENADE . FOUR A.M. THE USUAL . I HAD TO GO . I JUST HAD TO GO . IT WAS COLD . THERE WAS NO TRAFFIC . YOU UNLEASHED ME .

I DREAMED YOU SOLD US OUT . JOHN . IT WAS ON SUNDAY . HUSHED AND BLUE . WITH PUDDLES OF DOVES ON THE SIDEWALK . THAT WENT COO . AND UNDER BLUE BALLOONS . OF SKY HIGH . OVER THE AIR . YOU SOLD US OUT IN WASHINGTON SQUARE . JUST AS IF WE WEREN'T THERE .

SEE YOURSELF AS A SUCKER . ROSE . YOU'VE LEFT THE ART WORLD . WHAT ARE YOUR LIES WORTH NOW .

THE DOG STUDIES COST ACCOUNTING .

I HAVE NOTHING TO HIDE . NINETY NINE . NINETY EIGHT .

HOW DID YOU UNLEASH ME . JOHN . CAN YOU RECALL . WHY WITH A SMILE . OF COURSE . AND I . I WAS TO BOUND AHEAD . TAIL ALL ATWITTER . STICK MY NOSE IN THE NEAREST TURD . I GUESS I WAS SUPPOSED TO GET OFF ON IT . THIS GIFT OF FREE REIN .

WELL I DIDN'T . IT WAS ALL ABOUT YOUR IMAGE . AND I DETESTED IT . TO BE LEASHED ACCORDS ONE THE RESPECT OF THE PRISONER . TO BE TRAILED ALONG ON A PAVLOVIAN RUBBER BAND ACCORDS ONE THE PITY OF THE DAMNED .

YOU ARE A SUBTLE MAN . REFINED ENOUGH TO FILTER THROUGH ALL MANNER OF FINE SELVES . SAVE MINE . THE FILTER OF MISTRUST . I WAS PETRIFIED . ON THE LOOSE . I ACTUALLY DOGGED YOUR FOOTSTEPS . PARANOIA RAN AWAY WITH MY MIND . WERE YOU TELLING ME SOMETHING . DID YOU WANT ME TO . JUST GET LOST .

WE WENT TO THE ALL NIGHT FRUIT STAND . I WOULDN'T LEAVE YOU LONG ENOUGH TO PISS ON THE SNOW . YOU TOLD ME . STAY . I STAYED . I SAT LIKE A STONE IN A PUDDLE . YOU CAME OUT WITH A HUNDRED THOUSAND DOLLAR BAR AND THREW ME A PIECE . YOU SAID . CATCH . I OPENED MY MOUTH IN ASTONISHMENT . BECAUSE RIGHT THERE . IN MIDAIR . I GOT IT .

JOHN I SAID . I HATE ONE HUNDRED THOUSAND DOLLAR BARS . I SPIT IT AT A PARKING METER . YOU DIDN'T ANSWER ME . YOU STUCK TWO FINGERS IN YOUR MOUTH AND WHISTLED .

I COULD NOT SUPPRESS A SMILE . IN A WAVE OF GENEROSITY . THAT CAN BE LIKENED ONLY TO A WAVE OF LOVE . MY HEART DECLARED YOU WINNER BY DEFAULT . YES BOSS I SAID . AND CAME ON THE TROT . ACTUALLY IT WAS KIND OF A SOFT SHOE . YOU LOOKED LIKE SUCH A

I'VE NEVER FELT LIKE THIS BEFORE . FOUR SIXTY FIVE .

I'LL NEVER FEEL LIKE THIS AGAIN . BUY ONE . GET THE SECOND FREE .

I CAN TAKE ANYTHING . THREE FIFTY A WEEK . LESS THE SOCIAL SECURITY .

I'LL PAY TOMORROW . TWO BITS .

LET'S WORK TOGETHER . FOUR THOUSAND IN LEGAL FEES .

THIS IS EMBARRASSING . FIFTY . FIFTY .

WHAT A WAY TO MAKE A LIVING .

I DON'T WANT TO FUCK YOU OVER . ANY SIX FIGURE FIGURE .

124 CUNT . YOU LOOKED LIKE A STRAIGHT MAN . BOSS . I SAID . I GOT THE MESSAGE . THIS IS NIGHT SCHOOL . YOU'RE TRAINING ME TO BE A DOG .

YOU LOOKED AT ME . IT WAS A LOOK . LIKE THE LOOK . YOU USED TO LOOK . WHEN IT LOOKED LIKE YOU SAW ME .

THEN YOU SPOKE TO ME . YOU SAID . HEEL GIRL . YOU'RE A SUBTLE MAN . I'M MORE DIRECT BY NATURE . I SAID . NO JOHN . YOU'RE THE HEEL .

YOU SAID . ROSE . LISTEN TO ME . ROSE . THIS CAN'T GO ON . I SAID . JOHN . LISTEN TO ME . JOHN . THIS CAN'T GO ON . YOU SAID . ROSE . WHAT DO YOU WANT FROM ME . I SAID . JOHN . WHAT DO YOU WANT FROM ME . YOU SAID . JUST DON'T PUT ME ON . I SAID . JUST DON'T PUT ME ON . YOU SAID . I'M WARNING YOU . DON'T MAKE ME MAD . I SAID . I'M WARNING YOU . DON'T MAKE ME MAD .

YOU RAISED YOUR HAND TO ME . I BARED MY TEETH TO YOU . YOU WHACKED MY BUN . I BIT YOUR THUMB . I BIT THE HAND THAT FED ME . JUST FOR THAT . MY ASS YOU STOMPED . AND JUST FOR THAT YOUR FOOT I CHOMPED .

OH BABY IT WAS DOG EAT DOG .

MY LIFE SUCKS . SIX SIXTY SIX . IT'S THE BEAST .

YOU SAID . IT'S DOG EAT DOG . I SAID . IT'S DOG EAT DOG . WE SAID .
I'M NO DOG . YOU SAID . LIE . I SAID . LIE . YOU SAID . OUR LIFE
TOGETHER HAS BEEN ONE BIG LIE . I SAID . OUR LIFE TOGETHER HAS
BEEN ONE BIG LIE . YOU SAID . YOU SAID IT . I SAID . YOU SAID IT .
YOU SAID . YOU CAN'T DISTINGUISH ANY MORE BETWEEN YOUR
FANTASIES AND WHAT IS REAL . I SAID . YOU CAN'T DISTINGUISH ANY
MORE BETWEEN YOUR FANTASIES AND WHAT IS REAL . YOU SAID .
THAT'S THE LEGAL DEFINITION OF INSANE . I SAID. THAT'S THE LEGAL
DEFINITION OF INSANE . YOU SAID . ACCORDING TO THE LAW I'M
DEALING WITH A MAD DOG . I SAID . ACCORDING TO THE LAW I'M
DEALING WITH A MAD DOG. YOU SAID . I'M NOT GOING TO STAND ON
SOME STREET CORNER AT FOUR A.M. AND LET SOME TWITCHY BITCH
SCREAM AT ME THAT I'M CRAZY . THIS IS THE BOTTOM LINE . I
SAID . ASSHOLE . THERE IS NO BOTTOM LINE .

I FLASHED .

I . . . FLASHED ON THIS . . . RECTANGLE . IT WAS TENSE . KIND OF
A . . . SPEED THING . IN THE . . . CENTER . WITH . WITH THIS LAID
BACK THING . ALL AROUND IT . VERY . . . VERY VERY FRAIL . I DON'T
THINK . YOU KNOW . . . HOW FRAIL THESE . . . . . ARE IN THE
BEGINNING . . . CHANGES INSIDE . IN . . . SIDE I FLASHED ON A
RECTANGLE WITH 666 LINE HORIZONTAL RESOLUTION . AND INSIDE .
THE RECTANGLE . IN THE VERY CENTER OF . . . THE THING . WAS
TELLY . AND HE SAID . SWEETS . THEY'VE MOVED IN ON GARBAGE .

HALF A BLOCK DOWN A GARBAGE TRUCK WAS GRINDING UP A
MATTRESS . IT WAS A GREEN MACK WITH BONNANO AND SONS
LETTERED ON THE BUMPER . ABOVE . WATCH OUT . SCHOOLS IN .

THE WORD IS STUPID .

THE DOG IDENTIFIES HER LIVING
ROOM WITH THE VAMPIRE OF
STUPIDITY .

IN THIS AWE INSPIRING PLACE .
WHERE YOU ARE PERFECTLY
ENDOWED . WITH IGNORANCE .
NOTE ON YOUR LEDGER . OPPOSITE
EXPENDITURES . THE CREDIT OF A
VISION . A CUR . AT A GARBAGE
PIT . A PICTURE OF YOUR MIND .

126 HERE IT COMES . A SANITATION ENGINEER WAS RIDING ON THE RUNNING BOARD . I SAID . THEN THIS IS IT . THIS IS THE HIT . YOU SAID . OH SHIT .

I WENT FOR YOUR WRIST . STEPPED IN . BIT DOWN . FLIPPED MY HIP . AND THREW YOU FACE DOWN ON THE SIDEWALK . THANKS TO MY K9 COMMAND TRAINING I WAS ON TOP OF IT . YOU LOOKED UP AT ME . LIKE A NAUGHTY DOG . LIKE A DESPICABLE DOG . YOUR EARS WERE BACK . YOUR EYES WERE CLOSED . YOU TRIED TO CRAWL INTO A SIDEWALK CRACK . YOUR BACK BONE BENT UNTIL IT WAS A WISH BONE AND YOUR TAIL CURLED UP LIKE TOILET PAPER ON A ROLL . I PICKED YOU UP BY THE SCRUFF OF THE NECK . YOU WERE GUILTY . MAN . YOU WERE A PICTURE OF GUILT . I SAID . I KNOW A SANITATION ENGINEER WHEN I SEE A SANITATION ENGINEER . THOSE GUYS ARE HIT MEN . MAN . THOSE GUYS WERE FLOWN IN FROM DETROIT . RIGHT . YOU SAID . WRONG . CLEVELAND . I SAID . YOU PUT A CONTRACT OUT ON ME . YOU BOUGHT THE BIG BITE . RIGHT . YOU SAID . WRONG . IT WAS ALL LESLIE'S IDEA . I SAID . TAKING ME FOR A RIDE . YOU SAID . A WALK . I SAID . WALKING THE DOG . JUST GIVE ME THE FACTS . RELAX YOU SAID . EX LAX . EVERY MORNING . FOUR A.M. YOU'D HAVE TO GO . THERE WAS A PLOT . I SAID . YOU SANK THAT LOW . YOU SAID . LOWER . THERE WAS A SUB PLOT . I SAID . DOGGIE SCHOOL . YOU SAID . IF WE COULD PROVE YOU A DOG IN A COURT OF LAW WE'D BEAT THE RAP . JOHN . I SAID . WOW . I SAID . OH JOHN . OH WOW . I SAID . BOW WOW .

I LOOKED INTO YOUR EYES . YOUR GUILTY EYES . AND I DIDN'T KNOW WHO I WAS LOOKING AT . I WAS COMPLETELY TAKEN ABACK . I WAS TAKEN SO FAR ABACK . I BACKED OFF THE CURB INTO THE MIDDLE OF SECOND AVENUE . WHERE I SAT DOWN AND STARTED WORKING ON A FLEA . YOU SAT DOWN BESIDE ME ON A MANHOLE COVER . AND STARTED READING THE **ENQUIRER** .

SEE YOURSELF AS A SUCKER . ROSE . THERE'S A STRAW IN YOUR MOUTH . IT'S YOUR LAST STRAW . THERE'S A LOLLIPOP IN THE FREEZER . LOOK AT THE DETAIL .

I SAID . GET OFF THE MANHOLE COVER . MAN . STEAM ROSE AROUND
US . I COULD . FEEL IT COMING . FOAM IN MY MOUTH . BLOOD IN MY
EYE . I SAID . JOHN . I'M MAKING MY MOVE . YOU SAID . OUT OF THE
CROSSWALK . I SAID . OVER THE LINE . YOU LOOKED AT ME LIKE I
WAS CRAZY . I SAID . VERY CLEVER . LOOKING AT ME LIKE I'M
CRAZY . YOU SAID . YOU'RE A SICK DOG . ROSE . YOU'RE SICK AS A
DOG CAN BE .

THE GARBAGE TRUCK WAS SHIFTING RIGHT THROUGH ALL ITS TWENTY
SEVEN GEARS . IT WAS A HIT ALRIGHT . IT WAS A HIT AND RUN .
ROSE . YOU PLEADED . COME ON GIRL . COME BACK AND WE CAN PUT
IT ALL TOGETHER . LESLIE'S SLEEPING . YOU CAN COME ON HOME AND
EAT MY SHIT . IF YOU DO IT QUIETLY . I SAID . JOHN . DON'T TEMPT
ME .

I FOAMED . I BIT MY WRISTS . MY PAWS . MY TICKS . I WENT INTO
CONVULSIONS . THIS WAS REALLY PAINFUL . YOU SEE . ALL ALONG I'D
NEVER DOUBTED THERE'D BE SOMETHING IN ALL THIS FOR ME . SOME
BASIC HUMAN CONSIDERATION . BUT ALL ALONG I'D BEEN DEAD .
WRONG . IT WAS PURE MADNESS . YOU SEE JOHN . ALL ALONG I HAD
THESE YEARNINGS . I CONFESS NOW . I HAD UPWARDLY MOBILE
YEARNINGS . A BACK YARD . A LITTLE LIFE INSURANCE . ALL ALONG I
DREAMED . OF LIFE . SOMEWHERE . WHERE I COULD HOLD MY HEAD UP .
ALL ALONG I DREAMED OF HOLDING MY HEAD UP . ABOUT FIVE FOOT
FIVE . WITH HEELS . BUT ALL ALONG . I'D BEEN DEAD WRONG . IT WAS
PURE MADNESS .
I WANTED SOMEBODY UP THERE TO LOVE ME . SOMEBODY HIGH ABOVE
ALL ANIMAL KIND . I WAS A KARMIC STAR FUCKER . ALL ALONG I
THOUGHT THAT I COULD SUCK UP TO A STATE OF GRACE . BUT ALL
ALONG . I'D BEEN DEAD WRONG . I SUCKED YOU DOWN . IT WAS PURE
MADNESS .

I WAS SO BLIND . AND SO AMBITIOUS . HERE WAS LOVE . DOWN HERE .
HE'S STILL BAYING AT MY WINDOW FROM HIS BENCH IN WINO PARK .
BUT NO . BROADWAY WAS TOO CLOSE . JOHN . TOO CLOSE TO THE
GROUND . NO . I WAS SAVING MYSELF FOR A CHANCE AT THE BIG TIME
. A CHANCE TO CHANGE . MASTER . IN ONE LIFETIME . FROM YOUR
DOG . INTO YOUR MISTRESS .

I'M ASHAMED OF MY SOUL . DOGS . FORGIVE ME . I'M ASHAMED OF
MY SOUL . I'M GOING TO FREE IT . SO IT CAN RUN AWAY AND HIDE .

I CLOSED MY EYES . AND OPENED MY MIND . DEATH'S ENGINE WOULD
NOT FIND ME UNPREPARED . I HEARD A GRIND AND A ROAR AND A
VALVE KNOCK . IT WAS CLOSE NOW . I HEARD TWO MISSING TEETH IN
THE TRANSMISSION . AND SOMETHING ELSE WAS MISSING .

I CLOSED MY MIND AND OPENED MY EYES . THE FUCKING GARBAGE
TRUCK WAS MISSING ME BY A MILE . SCREW IT . WHO NEEDS IT . I
HAD ALL I NEEDED . I'D SNUFF MYSELF ON MY BROKEN HEART . I
COMPOSED MY SOUL . THEN I COMPOSED MY EPITAPH . **TOO MANY
PARTIES** .

YOU'VE LEFT THE ART WORLD .
ROSE . WHAT ARE YOUR LIES
WORTH NOW .

A TOKEN . OF THE WILL TO WAIT .

BECAUSE YOU CANNOT WAIT
UNOCCUPIED . I WILL CREATE
TECHNIQUES FOR YOU TO WAIT
WITH .

I WILL MARK OUT SPACES . I WILL
MAKE DEVICES . I WILL GIVE YOU A
LOVE TO PLAY WITH . AND A LITTLE
PLAY TO LOVE . I'LL WRITE IT
MYSELF .

BECAUSE YOU CANNOT WAIT
UNOCCUPIED . I GIVE YOU ALL THIS
MATERIAL .

THIS HOT WIND . THAT IS A LITTLE
CRAZY . THIS BEAUTIFUL DOLL .
THIS BODY . THIS ETHERIC BODY OF
YOUR IMAGINATION .

AND FINE TUNING . FOR YOUR
STEREO . AND NEXT YEAR IF
YOU'RE A GOOD GIRL . COLOR FOR
YOUR VIDEO .

ANYTHING YOU WANT . YOU WRITE
TO ME . CARE OF THE NORTH
POLE .

BECAUSE YOU CANNOT WAIT
UNOCCUPIED . I WILL MAKE A
PROGRESS .

A LITTLE TUNNEL . WITH A LITTLE
LIGHT WAY AT THE END . YOU CAN
ASSEMBLE IT YOURSELF . JUST
FOLLOW THE DIRECTIONS . THEN
YOU'LL HAVE IT . YOUR WORK .
CUT OUT FOR YOU . IT WILL
BECOME A WAITING .

MERRY CHRISTMAS .

UNOBSERVED . THE DOG SEES
HERSELF DUMPING HER GARBAGE .

130 I CAME TO IN YOUR ARMS . MUSIC WAS PLAYING . IT CAME FROM THE GARBAGE TRUCK . FROM A PANASONIC C105 3 HEAD CASSETTE RECORDER ON THE DASH BOARD OF THE GARBAGE TRUCK . YOU HAD GATHERED ME UP . YOU TOOK ME . FOR WHAT I WAS . YOUR GARBAGE .

IT WASN'T EXACTLY IN YOUR ARMS . IT WAS BY THE TAIL LIKE A DEAD RAT . OVER THE REFUSE COMPRESSOR . OVER THE MAW . WHICH WAS CHEWING UP AN EARLY AMERICAN COFFEE TABLE WITH A BULLET HOLE IN THE LEG . I LOOKED UP AT YOUR EYES . END OF SHAGGY DOG . I SAID . YOU COULDN'T ANSWER ME . YOU WERE ALL CHOKED UP . I SAID . YOU'RE NO DOG . YOU'RE A CHICKEN .

YOU STARTED TO CRY . AND COVER ME WITH KISSES . I PRIED YOUR HAND AWAY AND LICKED YOU ON THE FOREHEAD . GOODBYE . DEAR . I SAID . AND SANK INTO THE NIGHT LIKE A PIECE OF BACON IN A BOWL OF SPLIT PEA SOUP . I LOVE YOU ROSE . YOU CRIED . INTO THE WAVE OF SPLIT PEA NIGHT THAT COVERED ME . I LOVE YOU JOHN . I CALLED .

WHY . YOU CRIED . WHY ROSE . TOO MUCH PAIN . NO JOHN . I CALLED . TOO MUCH VAIN . END OF SHAGGY DOG . YOU SAID . I SAID . PART II BABY .

ROSE . LOOK AT THE SPACE YOU'VE CLEARED . CAN YOUR NEW LIFE COME AND LIVE WITH YOU . IS THERE ROOM . IS THERE TIME . ALL THAT OLD JAZZ .

WHERE HAVE YOU BEEN . JOHN . HAVE YOU BEEN OUT . ON THE
STREET POSTING SIGNS . IN THIS WEATHER . POOR DARLING . YOU'LL
CATCH YOUR DEATH OF COLD .

WHAT'S THAT ON YOUR PANTS . DID YOU SLIP . AND SPILL YOUR POT
OF GLUE . DON'T FRET . IT'LL ALL COME OUT IN THE WASH . YOU
COULD USE SOME CHEER . ABOUT A HALF A CUP . AND THEN SOME
BLUEING AFTER THE FIRST CYCLE .

LET'S SEE . WHAT DOES YOUR SIGN SAY . THIS TIME .

LOST DOG .

THAT'S WHAT IT SAID LAST TIME . AND THE TIME BEFORE .

I SEE YOU'VE UPPED THE REWARD AGAIN . TWO HUNDRED AND TWENTY
FIVE DOLLARS FOR INFO LEADING TO THE RECOVERY....

132 JOHN . WHERE COULD YOU GET TWO HUNDRED AND TWENTY FIVE
DOLLARS .

OH THAT WAS UNFAIR . I DO KNOW HOW RESOURCEFUL YOU ARE .
YOU'D BOUNCE A CHECK . AND THEN YOU'D COVER IT WITH A LOAN
FROM LESLIE . YOU'D TELL HER YOU NEEDED IT FOR A MEMBERSHIP TO
JACK LA LANNE . SO YOU COULD GET IT UP . FOR HER BIRTHDAY . I
REMEMBER LESLIE'S BIRTHDAY . JOHN . IT WAS BLACK FRIDAY . THE
ANNIVERSARY OF A LOSS OF ASSETS . IN THE MATERIAL WORLD .

JOHN . DEAR ONE . THAT PICTURE OF ME ON YOUR FLYER . IT'S THREE
YEARS OLD . I DON'T LOOK LIKE THAT . DEAR ONE . NO . IT'S NOT THE
XEROX . LET'S NOT LAY THE BLAME ON DISCOUNT DRUG . I JUST
DON'T LOOK LIKE THAT ANYMORE . TO SOMEONE LOOKING FOR ME .
WITH THAT PICTURE . I'D BE UNIDENTIFIABLE .

ISN'T IT A LITTLE LATE TO CALL THE POUND . BE JUST A TRIFLE
CAREFUL . NOW I DIDN'T SAY BE REASONABLE . JUST BE CAREFUL .
THEY CAN THINK YOU'RE JUST A LITTLE CRACKED . OVER THERE . BUT
YOU DON'T REALLY WANT THEM FINDING YOU SOME MIDNIGHT . OUT
IN THE PARK . SMELLING THE PISS ON THE LEAVES . THAT'S BELLEVUE
BABY . AND DESPITE THE MIRACLE OF DESPERATION . YOU'D NEVER
KNOW ME THERE . YOU JUST DON'T HAVE THE NOSE FOR IT .

I'M LOST TO YOU JOHN GREED . MORE'S THE PITY . YOU'RE LOST TO
YOURSELF .

DON'T CRY . DEAR ONE . NOT AGAIN . NOT ANOTHER DRIPPY NIGHT .
JACKING OFF AND CRYING . CRYING AND JACKING OFF .

I COULD COME BACK NOW . HOW EASY IT WOULD BE . FOR ME . TO
JUST COME BACK . TO YOU . I'M TEMPTED . ON A NIGHT LIKE THIS .
SOAKED TO THE SKIN AS YOU MOST CERTAINLY MUST BE . TO MARCH
RIGHT UP THE STAIRS WITH A NICE SPRING CHICKEN AND FIX YOU A
BOWL OF CHICKEN SOUP . I'M REALLY TEMPTED . TO GET RIGHT TO
WORK ON THAT COLD .

HOW EASY IT WOULD BE FOR ME . AND IT WOULD KILL YOU .

I'M TOO OLD FOR YOU NOW . I CAN'T FACE YOU . IT WOULD KILL YOU .
I DON'T KNOW HOW LONG IT'S BEEN SINCE I'VE SEEN YOU . I DON'T
WANT TO FIGURE IT OUT . THREE YEARS . MAYBE FOUR . YOU KNOW
I'LL NEVER LEARN TO COUNT . THAT'S JUST TOO NEW A TRICK FOR A
DOG MY AGE . HERE AT THE INSTITUTE WE REALLY DON'T ADMIT THE
PROBLEM . HERE WE TEND TO THINK THERE ARE NO NEW TRICKS IN
THE WHOLE WIDE WORLD .

LIFE AT THE INSTITUTE HAS BEEN FOR ME . IN MOST RESPECTS A
DOG'S LIFE . NOT OF COURSE WITHOUT ITS OWN ILLUSIONS . BUT A
FULL LIFE . UP IN THE MORNING . OUT FOR A CRAP IN THE GRASS . A
LITTLE GATE DUTY . DIGGING IN THE GARDEN . I WORK WITH MRS.
PEARSON . I DIG THE HOLES . SHE FILLS THEM . WE FANTASIZE
TOGETHER THAT WE'RE PLANTING FRUIT TREES . QUITE A FULL LIFE .
IN THE VERNACULAR OF BIOLOGICAL CHRONOLOGY . I THINK A DOG'S
LIFE IS APPROXIMATELY SEVEN TIMES AS FULL AS ANYTHING YOU'VE
KNOWN . I'VE LIVED SEVEN YEARS FOR EVERY ONE OF YOURS . SEVEN
TIMES OUR SEPARATION . JOHN . JUST THINK OF IT . BY NOW I'M OF
ANOTHER GENERATION .

HOW CAN I FACE YOU . I'M TOO OLD FOR YOU . IT WOULD KILL YOU.
JOHN . . .

134 JOHN . YOU'RE NOT GOING OUT AGAIN . TO WHISTLE THE DOORWAYS
AGAIN WHERE THE STRAYS GO IN OUT OF THE RAIN . EVEN THOUGH
YOU TELL YOURSELF IT'S FOR A HUNDRED THOUSAND DOLLAR BAR .
JOHN LOVE . IT'S NOT WORTH IT .

YOU MUST PULL YOURSELF TOGETHER . JOHN . YOU MUST FIND
SOMETHING . SOMEWHERE . DEEP IN SOME HOLE .

HERE AT THE INSTITUTE WE LISTEN TO THE RADIO . AND TAKE HOT
BATHS . AND READ OURSELVES TO SLEEP . MAYBE I COULD READ TO
YOU . I'M IN YOUR EYE . AFTER ALL . JUST LIKE AN EYELASH . ON THE
EYEBALL .

TOO BAD . DEAR . IF IT'S THAT BAD . IF YOU HAVE TO GO . WHY DON'T
YOU JUST TRY NOT TO TAKE THE LEASH ALONG . TRY SOMETHING
SMALL . OH MY POOR UNHAPPY DARLING . I KNOW WHAT YOU DO WITH
IT . YOU DANGLE THE COLLAR OVER THE CURB JUST LIKE A NOOSE .
AND DRAG IT THROUGH THE GUTTER . THE PICTURE OF IT MAKES MY
HACKLES RISE . WALKING THE GHOST .

JOHN . DOES THE GHOST NEED WALKING .

THE WAGES OF ATTACHMENT . JOHN HOW HEAVY THEY WEIGH ON YOUR
MIND . DEAR ONE . BEWARE YOUR MIND . YOU'VE COME TO GRIEF .

I SEE NOW . HOW I SAW . HOW LOVE COULD COME TO PASS . THE
VERY NIGHT . I SLIPPED AWAY . HOW LONG AGO . FOR ME . FOR YOU .
JUST YESTERDAY . HOW UNBEKNOWNST . MY MIND SLIPPED BACK TO
YOU . AND LEFT A DEAR JOHN . BY A WATER DISH . I SEE NOW . HOW I
SLIPPED INTO A FANTASY . THAT YOU'D BE SORRY . SO VERY SORRY .
AND THAT YOU'D PAY . I SAW . YOU'D GET JUST WHAT YOU GAVE . AND

STARVE TO DEATH . I SEE I FED MYSELF . I TOLD MYSELF . YOU'D
COME TO SEE . THE VISTAS OF NOSTALGIA . THROUGH THE SOCKETS OF
DISDAIN . OH JOHN . OH HERE YOU ARE . YOU'VE COME TO PAIN .

YOU'VE COME AROUND . DEAR ONE . AROUND TO RUE . REGRET .
REMORSE . YOU'VE COME TO GRIPS . WITHOUT YOUR GLOVES . NO
WISDOM . NO REVELATION . NOT EVEN AN INSTINCT FOR SELF
PRESERVATION . YOU'VE COME A LONG WAY . HOME . TO ME . JOHN .
YOU'VE COME DOWN . TO A ROMANTIC . BABY . BELIEVE IT OR NOT .
YOU'VE COME TO BE BORN AGAIN . BABY . WHAT A CHEAP SHOT .

JOHN AT PAY PHONES I AND II

I
DIALS
JOHN'S ANONYMOUS . WELL LOOK
IN THE COMMERCIAL LISTINGS .
MANHATTAN . THANK YOU .

I
DIALS
HELLO . THIS IS JOHN . HANG ON
A SEC .

II
DIALS

I

WHILE II IS RINGING

HI . OH PRETTY GOOD . YEAH . I
GOT THE CARD ABOUT THE
MEETING BUT I WAS OVERLOADED
AT THE TIME . YEAH . WORK .
HANG ON A SEC .

II

HI . OH. I DIDN'T KNOW IT WAS
THAT LATE . NO . I DON'T HAVE A
WATCH . I HAVE AN ELECTRIC
ALARM CLOCK . WELL I WAS JUST
OUT ON THE STREET AND I
THOUGHT I'D DROP OVER
BUT . . . . I WOKE UP YOU YOUR
KITTENS .

I

I CAN'T DO IT .

II

HANG ON A SEC .

I

HI . SORRY . I CAN'T DO IT . NO . I
READ THAT BOOK . RIGHT . THE J.A.
MANUAL . THAT'S A LUCID BOOK .

YOU KNOW WHAT I'M SAYING .
THAT'S A WORK BOOK . RIGHT .
IT'S ABOUT WORK . YOU KNOW
WHAT I'M SAYING . NO . RIGHT .
I'M SAYING NO . YOU KNOW WHAT
I'M SAYING . MY THING IS NOT
ABOUT WORK . MY THING IS ABOUT
A VACATION . IN MY LIFE . AT A
CRITICAL JUNCTURE . I VOWED NOT
TO WORK . A DAY IN MY LIFE .
NO . THAT'S NOT THE POINT . THE
POINT IS . I CAN WORK . BUT I CAN
ONLY WORK WHEN IT'S A VACATION
FROM A VACATION . YOU KNOW
WHAT I'M SAYING . I'M SAYING I
CAN'T DO IT . IT JUST AIN'T
TOURISM . HANG ON A SEC .

II
HI . SORRY . WHEN DID YOU HAVE
KITTENS . YOU DIDN'T HAVE
KITTENS THE LAST TIME I SAW
YOU . NO . YOU WERE
UNATTACHED . NO THAT'S NOT THE
POINT . THE POINT IS . YOU HAD
KITTENS AND
YOU NEVER CALLED ME .
HANGS UP .
■
YOU GOT A DIME . THANKS . MAN .

138

II
DIALS
RING
TAPE
(HI . I'M NOT AT HOME RIGHT
NOW . BUT IF YOU'LL LEAVE YOUR
NUMBER AFTER THE BEEP ETC.)

I
DURING DIAL RING AND TAPE
HI . SORRY . WHAT DO YOU MEAN
I'M IN BAD SHAPE . I'VE BEEN
WORKING OUT . WHAT . WORK IN .
YOU DON'T KNOW WHAT YOU'RE
ASKING . YOU KNOW WHAT I'M
SAYING .

II
TAPE BEEP

I
HANG ON A SEC .

II
HI . THIS IS JOHN .
IF YOU PLAY YOUR TAPE WHEN
YOU GET HOME . WHY
DON'T YOU COME OVER . YOU
COULD JUST HOP IN A CAB AND ...

I

ADDITIONAL FIVE CENTS RECORDING

II

HANG ON A SEC .

I

OVER RECORDING
WHAT . I'M ON THE STREET .
YOU'LL CALL ME . I DON'T KNOW
THE NUMBER . HANG ON A SEC .

■

YOU GOT THE NUMBER .

I

I CAN'T READ THE NUMBER .

■

YOU GOT THE NUMBER .

I

I CAN'T READ THE NUMBER .

■

YOU GOT A LIGHT .

I
CLICKS DEAD

II
SORRY . NOW REMEMBER THE
BUZZER DOESN'T WORK . SO I'LL
PUT THE KEY IN A LUMINOUS
SOCK . SO WHEN YOU . . .
TAPE BEEP

■
YOU GOT A DIME .
■
YOU GOT ANOTHER DIME .
■
THANKS . MAN . THANKS . MAN .

I AND II
DIALS TOGETHER

I
WHILE II RINGS
HI . SORRY . I'M HAVING A
SEIZURE . THAT'S ALL . YOU DON'T
UNDERSTAND . I LIVE ON THE
EDGE .
OVER II
TAPE
YOU'RE COMING FOR ME . RIGHT . I
SHOULD STAY GLUED TO THE
CORNER .

■
DO YOU RECALL THE NAME OF THE
CORNER .

‖
TAPE BEEP

■
HANG ON A SEC .

‖
I NEGLECTED TO MENTION . UH .
WHY DON'T YOU BRING A BOTTLE
OF JD . OR A BOTTLE OF VO . OR A
BOTTLE OF VSOP . A COUPLE OF
STEAKS . SOME IDAHO POTATOES .
ICEBERG LETTUCE .
POLYUNSATURATED VEGETABLE
OIL . I'VE GOT THE VINEGAR .
HANGS UP

I
HI . SORRY . I CAN'T RECALL THE
NAME OF THE CORNER . I'LL HANG
ON .

■
YOU GOT A DIME .

I

CONTINUING

YOU KNOW SOMETHING . ONCE I
WAS A NOTHING . ISN'T THAT
SOMETHING .

■

THANKS . MAN .

I

CONTINUING

NO . I DON'T RECALL THE
DETAILS . RIGHT . SO TO SPEAK .
MY LIFE HAD ESCAPED MY
NOTICE . I WAS SUCH A NOTHING .
I WAS IN A STATE OF
ILLUMINATION .

DIALING II

UH HUH . SO TO SPEAK . I KNEW
THE TRIP . I KNEW THE BIT . I
KNEW THE MAN . I EVEN KNEW
THE NUMBER .

II RINGING

NOW WHAT I'M SAYNG IS . PUT
YOURSELF IN MY POSITION . IF
YOU KNEW . WHAT I KNEW .
WOULDN'T YOU KNOW YOU NEEDED
A VACATION .

II

TAPE

HANG ON A SEC .

WOULD YOU MIND BRINGING A
PLUNGER . THE JOHN IS BACKING
UP . I WOULDN'T ASK YOU . BUT
SINCE YOU'RE TAKING A CAB . YOU
KNOW WHAT I'M SAYING .
HANGS UP

I

HI . SORRY . I SAID . WOULDN'T
YOU KNOW YOU NEEDED A
VACATION . A KIND OF A **VIE EN
ROSE** . YOU KNOW WHAT I'M
SAYING . A KIND OF A **VIE EN ROSE**
UNDER A SORT OF A **CASABLANCA** LAP
DISSOLVED OVER A **DEEP THROAT** .
RIGHT . A COMPLETE VACATION
PACKAGE . THAT'S MY POINT . ALL
WORK AND NO PLAY MAKES JOHN
A DULL DICK . SO TO SPEAK . AM I
GETTING OVER YOUR HEAD .
GOOD . GOOD . JUST CHECKING .

NOW I'M A SHOOTER . BY
PROFESSION . I MEAN I'M A
STRAIGHT SHOOTER . MY
PROBLEMS LIE IN THE AREA OF
PROJECTION . I REMEMBER ONCE
PROJECTING **A PLACE IN THE SUN** ONTO
LESLIE . I MADE A MISTAKE . NO .
THAT'S NOT THE POINT . IT WAS A
CONCEPTUAL ERROR . THAT

SURFACE WAS RESERVED . FOR **THE BRIDE OF FRANKENSTEIN** . AND THEN THERE WAS MY OPTICAL SOUND TRACK . MY **VIE EN ROSE** . I PROJECTED THAT ONTO MY DOG . WELL IT'S AN OPTICAL SOUND TRACK . NO . THE PROBLEM WAS . THIS SMALL DOMESTIC ANIMAL STARTED PROJECTING RIGHT BACK ON ME .

I WAS PERCEIVED . I PERCEIVED MYSELF PERCEIVED . RIGHT . I PERCEIVED I WAS NOT JUST SOME TOM DICK OR HARRY . NO . I WAS A JOHN . RIGHT . I PERCEIVED THAT I . MYSELF . WAS NOT A SELF SUPPORTING SYSTEM . I WAS A REACTIVE SYSTEM . I FOLLOWED THE ACTION . ALL I NEEDED WAS A LITTLE ACTION . I FOLLOWED OTHER DOGS . I PANNED AROUND LOOKING FOR LITTLE PUSSY CATS . I ZOOMED IN ON A GERBIL ONCE BECAUSE SHE THOUGHT I LOOKED LIKE STEVE MCQUEEN . THEN I REALIZED THAT MY SHOOTING WAS AFFECTED .

I DISCOVERED THAT MY SHOOTING WAS AFFECTED SHOOTING A LONG

SHOT ON TWENTY THIRD STREET .
FORMERLY . WHEN SHOOTING .
LIGHT ENTERED MY APERTURE .
THROUGH MY LENS . AND LEFT AN
IMAGE RIGHT BETWEEN MY
SPROCKET HOLES . BUT NOW . MY
LIGHT . GOES THROUGH MY LENS
THE OTHER WAY . AND LEAVES MY
IMAGE ON TWENTY THIRD STREET .
THIS WAS DETAILED IN AN ARTICLE
BY ANNETTE MICHELSON CALLED
THE GREED EFFECT . THAT'S HOW IT'S
REFERRED TO IN THE INDUSTRY
TODAY . IN OTHER CIRCLES IT'S
CALLED THE MIRACLE OF TWENTY
THIRD STREET . IT
DEPENDS ON YOUR CIRCLE .

WELL FRANKLY I HAD A CREATIVE
CRISIS . THREE SHOTS A DAY .
THEN TWO . FOR A WHILE THERE I
WAS DOWN TO EIGHTEEN FRAMES A
WEEK ON SUNDAY AFTERNOONS .
THEN I CUT OUT COLOR . THERE I
WAS . DOWN TO BLACK AND
WHITE . I'D WAKE UP IN THE
MORNING WITH THE SHAKES . MY
HAIR CAME OUT . I WENT ON A
BENDER . I SHOT TWO REELS OF
TODD AO WITH QUADRAPHONIC
SOUND . AFTERWARDS I WAS
HOSPITALIZED .

I EMERGED FROM THE HOSPITAL A
CHANGED JOHN . I WAS A MARK .
YOU'RE A JUNKIE . JOHN . THEY
TOLD ME . YOU'VE GOT TO GO COLD
COCK . I SAID . I CAN'T DO IT .
DOC . I'VE FOUND MYSELF . I'M
HOOKED . ON MY REALITY . NOW .
I'M AFRAID . TO FADE . MY SELF .
IS MY VACATION .

WHAT CAN I DO . I GO INTO
MYSELF . I BECOME SELF
INVOLVED . I TRY TO BE SELF
EFFACING . BUT THAT'S SELF
DEFEATING . I INDULGE IN SELF
RECRIMINATION . BUT ALL THAT
DOES IS MAKE ME MORE SELF
CENTERED . I LONG TO BE SELF
TRANSCENDING . BUT THIS
BECOMES TOO SELF DELUDING .
WHICH BRINGS ME TO THE BRINK
OF SELF DESTRUCTION . WHICH
BECOMES A SUBJECT OF SELF
CONCERN . AM I BEING SELF
INDULGENT . GOOD . GOOD . JUST
CHECKING .

YOU GOT TO HELP ME . MAN . I'M
GOING DOWN THE GARDEN PATH .
SELF ASSERTION . THEN . SELF
DIRECTION . THEN . I GET JUST
PLAIN OLD SELFISH . AFTER WHICH

JOHN . LET ME TELL YOU THE STORY OF MY LIFE MY FUCKING DID NOT
START UNTIL AFTER I WAS THIRTY FIVE AND A FAIRLY SUCCESSFUL
CAREER HAD BEEN ESTABLISHED BUT SUCCESS BROUGHT INCREASED
SOCIAL ACTIVITIES AND I REALIZED THAT MANY OF MY FRIENDS
ENJOYED A SOCIAL FUCK WITH NO APPARENT HARM TO THEMSELVES
OR OTHERS I BEGAN TO JOIN THEM OCCASIONALLY I DISLIKED BEING
DIFFERENT AND AT FIRST IT WAS JUST THAT AN OCCASIONAL FUCK
THEN I STARTED LOOKING FORWARD TO MY WEEKEND GOLF AND THE
NINETEENTH HOLE GRADUALLY THE QUANTITY INCREASED THE
OCCASIONS FOR FUCKING CAME MORE FREQUENTLY A HARD DAY
WORRIES AND PRESSURE BAD NEWS GOOD NEWS THERE WERE MORE
AND MORE REASONS TO FUCK IT WAS FRIGHTENING FUCKING WAS
BEING SUBSTITUTED FOR MORE AND MORE OF THE THINGS I REALLY
ENJOYED DOING GOLF HUNTING AND FISHING WERE NOW MERELY
EXCUSES TO FUCK EXCESSIVELY I MADE PROMISES TO MYSELF MY
FAMILY AND FRIENDS AND BROKE THEM I TRIED TO HIDE MY FUCKING
BY GOING PLACES WHERE I WAS UNLIKELY TO SEE ANYONE I KNEW
REMORSE WAS ALWAYS WITH ME THE NEXT STEPS WERE CLOSET
FUCKING AND EXCUSES FOR TRIPS IN ORDER TO FUCK WITHOUT
RESTRAINT WHAT IT DOES TO A PERSON IS APPARENT TO EVERYONE
BUT THE PERSON INVOLVED WHEN IT BECAME NOTICEABLE TO THE
POINT OF COMMENT I DEVISED WAYS OF SNEAKING FUCKS ON THE SIDE
REHEARSALS BECAME PART OF THE PATTERN STOPPING TO FUCK ON
THE WAY TO A PLACE WHERE I WAS PLANNING TO FUCK NEVER HAVING
ENOUGH ALWAYS CRAVING MORE THE OBSESSION TO FUCK GRADUALLY
DOMINATED MY LIFE I TRIED CELIBACY ON NUMEROUS OCCASIONS BUT

FOLLOWETH . SELF SATISFACTION .
THAT'S THE PALE HORSE . MAN .
I'M ON THE EDGE . MAN . I'M ON
THE EDGE . OF BEING . A SELF
MADE . MAN .

■
YOU GOT ABOUT THIRTY FOUR
DOLLARS . I GOT TO CALL
LUXEMBOURG .
■
THANKS ANYWAY MY MAN . I'LL
CALL COLLECT .
■
YOU GOT A DIME . THANKS MAN .

‖
GET ME THE CABLE .
DIME COMES BACK
THANKS MAN . THE
TRANSATLANTIC CABLE .

‖
INFORMATZIONE LUXEMBOURG . JE
VOUDRAIT UNT NUMER TELEFOON .
SI . LIEBA STOED .
YAH . ES TAY OH OOH DAY . YAH .
O.K. BON D'ACCORD . MIT
UMLAUT . THANKS MY MAN .
ACHTUNG HEY ACHTUNG .
COLLECTARE .

148 I ALWAYS FELT UNHAPPY AND ABUSED I TRIED PSYCHIATRY BUT OF COURSE I GAVE THE PSYCHIATRIST NO COOPERATION I WAS LIVING IN CONSTANT FEAR THAT I WOULD GET CAUGHT FUCKING WHILE DRIVING A CAR SO I USED TAXIS EVENTUALLY MY ENTIRE PERSONALITY CHANGED TO A CYNICAL INTOLERANT AND ARROGANT PERSON COMPLETELY DIFFERENT FROM MY NORMAL SELF I RESENTED ANYONE AND EVERYONE WHO INTERFERED WITH MY PERSONAL PLANS I WAS FULL OF SELF PITY IT SEEMED TO ME MY WIFE WAS BECOMING MORE INTOLERANT AND NARROW MINDED ALL THE TIME WHENEVER WE WENT OUT SHE APPEARED TO GO OUT OF HER WAY TO KEEP ME FROM HAVING MORE THAN ONE FUCK SHE OF COURSE DIDN'T REALIZE HOW CUNNING A JOHN CAN BE OUR INVITATIONS BECAME FEWER AND FEWER WE HAD ENCOURAGED OUR CHILDREN TO BRING THEIR FRIENDS HOME AT ANY TIME BUT AFTER A FEW EXPERIENCES WITH A FUCKING FATHER THEY ELIMINATED HOME AS A PLACE TO ENTERTAIN I WILL NEVER KNOW ALL THE PEOPLE I HURT ALL THE FRIENDS I ABUSED THE HUMILIATION OF MY FAMILY WE THINK WE CAN FUCK TO EXCESS WITHOUT ANYONE KNOWING IT EVERYONE KNOWS IT . . .

BY MOONLIGHT IN LONELY PLACES NEAR THE SEA WHEN YOU ARE PLUNGED IN BITTER REFLECTIONS YOU SEE THAT EVERYTHING ASSUMES A YELLOWISH APPEARANCE . VAGUE . FANTASTIC . THE TREE SHADOWS . NOW SWIFT NOW SLOW . CHASE HITHER AND YON AS THEY FLATTEN THEMSELVES AGAINST THE EARTH . LONG AGO WHEN I WAS BORNE UPON THE WINGS OF YOUTH THIS SEEMED STRANGE TO ME AND MADE ME DREAM . NOW I AM USED TO IT . THE WIND MURMURS ITS LANGUOROUS STRAIN THROUGH THE LEAVES AND THE OWL INTONES HIS SAD COMPLAINT WHILE THE HAIR OF THOSE WHO HEAR STANDS ON END .

II
ALLO . PREGO . PRONTO . ATTENZIONE . WHAT'S HAPPENING . SHE WON'T ACCEPT . SHE REJECTS . MAN . SHE DON'T UNDERSTAND . I'M ON THE EDGE .

II
OH HI . SORRY . WHERE AM I . I'M ON THE STREET . WHERE ARE YOU . ON THE BIDET . SORRY . WELL . THE POINT IS . FREDDIE LAKER . I THOUGHT YOU KNEW FREDDIE LAKER . I THOUGHT I REMEMBERED YOU WERE INTIMATE WITH FREDDIE LAKER . WELL THAT'S THE POINT . RIGHT . I WAS WRONG . WELL THE POINT IS .

FOR YEARS I'VE BEEN CRUISING AND NOW I AM IN THE MARKET FOR AN ALTERNATIVE MODE OF TRANSPORTATION . AT A DISCOUNT . YEAH . . .

THEN INFURIATED DOGS SNAP THEIR CHAINS AND ESCAPE FROM
DISTANT FARMS . THEY RUSH THROUGH THE COUNTRYSIDE . HERE .
THERE AND EVERYWHERE . IN THE GRIP OF MADNESS . SUDDENLY
THEY STOP . TURN THEIR FIERY EYES IN ALL DIRECTIONS AND RAISE
THEIR HEADS . THEIR NECKS SWELL HORRIBLY . AND ONE BY ONE THEY
COMMENCE TO HOWL . LIKE A CHILD CRYING FROM HUNGER . OR A
WOMAN ABOUT TO BE DELIVERED OF A CHILD . OR A PLAGUE VICTIM
DYING . OR A YOUNG GIRL SINGING A DIVINE MELODY .

THE DOGS HOWL AT THE NORTHERN STARS . AT THE EASTERN STARS .
AT THE SOUTHERN STARS . AT THE WESTERN STARS . AT THE MOON .
AT THE SILENCE OF THE NIGHT . AT AN OWL WHOSE SLANTING FLIGHT
BRUSHES THE DOGS' MUZZLES . AT SNAKES RUSTLING IN THE BRIARS
MAKING THE DOGS' FLESH CREEP . AT THE KEEN AIR THEY BREATHE IN
DEEP LUNGFULS BURNING AND REDDENING THEIR NOSTRILS . AT THEIR
OWN HOWLINGS WHICH SCARE THEMSELVES . AT THE TREES WHOSE
GENTLY CRADLED LEAVES ARE SO MANY MYSTERIES THAT THE DOGS
CANNOT UNDERSTAND . AT THE ROCKS ON THE SHORE . AT THE LIGHTS
ON THE MASTS OF INVISIBLE VESSELS . AT THE HEAVY SOUND OF THE
SEA . AT THE GREAT FISH WHICH AS THEY SWIM REVEAL THEIR BLACK
BACKS BEFORE PLUNGING AGAIN IN THE DEPTHS . AND AT MAN WHO
MAKES SLAVES OUT OF DOGS .

AFTER THIS THEY SCAMPER OVER THE COUNTRYSIDE AGAIN . LEAPING
WITH THEIR BLEEDING FEET OVER DITCHES AND PATHWAYS FIELDS
PASTURES AND STEEP ROCKS . THEIR ENDLESS HOWLING HORRIFIES
NATURE . ALAS FOR THE WAYFARER . FOR THE DOGS WILL FLING
THEMSELVES UPON HIM . TEAR HIM TO PIECES . DEVOUR HIM WITH
THEIR BLOOD DRIPPING JAWS . FOR THE DOGS HAVE SHARP TEETH .
WILD ANIMALS NOT DARING TO INVITE THEMSELVES TO SHARE THIS

FEAST OF FLESH HASTEN TREMBLING AWAY . AFTER MANY HOURS THE
DOGS WEARY OF RACING HITHER AND YON ALMOST EXPIRING . THEIR
TONGUES LOLLING OUT OF THEIR MOUTHS . THROW THEMSELVES UPON
ONE ANOTHER NOT KNOWING WHAT THEY ARE DOING AND TEAR ONE
ANOTHER INTO A THOUSAND PIECES . THEY DO NOT BEHAVE THUS
FROM CRUELTY .

ONE DAY MY MOTHER HER EYES GLASSY LOOKING SAID TO ME . WHEN
YOU ARE IN BED AND YOU HEAR THE HOWLING OF THE DOGS IN THE
FIELDS . HIDE YOURSELF BENEATH YOUR BLANKETS . DON'T MAKE A
JEST OF WHAT THEY ARE DOING . THEY HAVE THE INSATIABLE THIRST
FOR THE INFINITE . LIKE YOU . LIKE ME . I WILL EVEN PERMIT YOU TO
STAND AT THE WINDOW AND SEE THIS SPECTACLE . WHICH IS RATHER
MAGNIFICENT .

THERE NOW JOHN . ASLEEP AT LAST . HOW SLEEP PLAYS FALSELY
WITH US STILL . A GAME IT HAS ALREADY WON . ARE YOU WITH ME
WITH YOUR EYES CLOSED . AM I WITH YOU . SEE NOW . NOW WE
DON'T LOOK . FOOLISH . DO WE .

THERE THERE NOW JOHN . I ALWAYS DID GET OFF ON READING YOU TO
SLEEP . ONE STORY AFTER ANOTHER . FAIRY TALES AND TRUE
CONFESSIONS . FIRST FACTS . AND SECOND FICTIONS . EVERY WORD
TRUE . THE TRUTH PUTS YOU TO SLEEP . I LEARNED THAT EARLY . I
LEARNED YOUR LULLABY . TRUE LOVE . TONIGHT IT TOOK SO LONG .
LONGER THAN USUAL .

WHAT WAS THE TROUBLE . JOHN . DEAR JOHN . WERE YOU EXTRA
HUNGRY . THAT'S IT I'LL BET . AND NOTHING IN THE ICE BOX . TOOK
YOUR FANCY . AND AS USUAL . YOU WERE TOO LAZY TO COOK .

IT TOOK SO LONG . I CAN'T EVEN REMEMBER HOW I STARTED . THIS
ONE . WHAT'D I SAY . GIVE ME A BREAK . BABY . FEED ME THE LINE .
DEAR JOHN . UH HUH . I SAID . GOOD BYE . TELL ME . WHAT'D I SAY .
DON'T LAUGH . DON'T CRY . WHAT'D I SAY NOW . MAYBE I CAN HELP
YOU . I SAID FAT CHANCE . TELL ME . WHAT'D I SAY . STILL WANT TO
LICK YOUR EYES. . ALRIGHT . I HAVE TO DEAL WITH THAT .

DROPPED BY THE VET TODAY . WE HAD A FRANK DISCUSSION .
BERNSTEIN IS PROGRESSIVE . HE HAD FACTS AND FIGURES . THERE
WAS NO ARGUING ON SCIENTIFIC GROUNDS . JUST DO IT . ROSE . HE
SAID . IT'S CHEAP AND PAINLESS . HOW CHEAP . I SAID . HE HAD A
CREDIT PLAN . HOW PAINLESS . I SAID HE SMOOTHED MY EARS . NOW
HOW LONG HAVE I KNOWN YOU ROSELE . YOU TRUST ME . YOU WON'T
FEEL A THING .

SHOULD I DO IT JOHN . WHAT DO YOU THINK . SHOULD I GET FIXED .
FOR GOOD .

I'M TRULY CONFUSED . TRUE LOVE . ON THE ONE HAND . LOATHE TO
ADMIT TO A MERE MEDICAL SOLUTION . ON THE OTHER . NO PERFECT
FOOL COULD FAIL TO SEE . A BIG FIX . AT THE CENTER OF MY THINKING .
ALL ALONG .

NOT TO FEEL A THING . FUNNY . HOW THAT DESCRIBES MY WORK .
HERE . AT THE INSTITUTE . I'M SHOCKED . AT SUCH A PERFECT TURN
OF PHRASE . I'M EASILY SHOCKED . OF LATE . WHEN LATE . INTO MY
WORKING HOURS . SOME JOKER COMES TO ME . AND PLAYS WITH ME .
MY FAVORITE GAME . WHEN IN MY WINTER MIND . SOME JOKER . SETS
A MATCH . TO MY FIREPLACE . HEART .

THEY COME TWICE A YEAR . I'M QUITE A REGULAR DOG . WHY IS IT
THEN . TRUE LOVE . THEY ALWAYS SEEM TO COME . JUST ONE MORE

152 TIME . AND LIKE A PALEOLITHIC SPRING . IN THE FOSSIL OF MY TUBE .
A STONE EGG DROPS . INTO A ROSE COLORED FOUNTAIN .

AND I'M IN HEAT AGAIN . BABY . I'M TYRANNIZED AGAIN . BABY .
FUNKY CHICKEN . LICKIN' . AGAIN . PRETTY BABY .

DO YOU REMEMBER MY FIRST HEAT . JOHN . HOW YOU GAVE ME A COLD
BATH . I WAS A BABY . DADDY . REMEMBER ME . A WET WORM . IN A
COLD BATH . YOU THOUGHT I WAS EMBARRASSED . WHAT A DUMB
PRICK YOU WERE . HOW ANY FOOL COULD FAIL TO SEE . THE THREAD
OF SILK I WAS UNWINDING . HOW ANY FOOL COULD FAIL TO SEE . THE
PERMANENCE OF FRAGILITY . HOW I . LIKE AN ION . WITH AN
UNBALANCED CHARGE . BORE A BOND . IN THE FIELD OF FORCE
CALLED RAPTURE .

I WAS ATTACHING . BABY .

WELL . HERE I GO AGAIN . CAN YOU BELIEVE IT . AT MY AGE . WOW .
CAN I BE FOR REAL . I MEAN REALLY . NOW . IF I DIDN'T KNOW
BETTER . I'D THINK I WAS FUCKED FOREVER . THEN AGAIN . KNOWING
WHAT I KNOW . I KNOW IT'S ONLY ABOUT SIX DAYS .

HERE I GO AGAIN . WHAT CAN I DO . WITH LOVE . FOR YOU . IT'S LIKE
A PIECE OF FURNITURE . TOO BIG FOR THE ROOM . WHERE CAN I PUT
IT . BABY . IT LOOKS BAD . I TRIP OVER IT . AND HURT MYSELF . I
CAN'T GET IT OUT THE DOOR . IT'S HEAVY METAL .

IT'S A LIE . SURE BABY . BUT WHO GIVES A FUCK . IT'S A MOVIE . IT'S
A HIT . BABY . BUT IT SUCKS . I TRY TO RECUT IT . USE MY SMARTS .
CAN'T YOU HEAR ME . SNIP . SNIP . CUT IT OUT . ROSE . CAN'T YOU
SEE . MY PERPLEXITY . LOOKING FOR THE FRAMES TO THROW AWAY .

I CAN CUT IT . HERE I GO IT AGAIN . NO . I CAN'T CUT IT . HERE I
BLOW IT . AGAIN . I KNOW IT. I NEED IT . BABY . ONE MORE TIME . I
WANT TO LOVE YOU BABY . ONE MORE TIME .

ONE MORE TIME I WHINE AND I WHIMPER . I SCRATCH ON YOUR DOOR .
HEY JACK SMACK . IT'S YOUR UNCLE SAM . I WANT . YOU . BABY .
ONLY YOU . WILL DO . IT . BABY . LIKE A DOG I'LL FIND YOU .
MASTER . FIND YOU OR STARVE . OH . LIKE A HOUND . I'LL BAY AT
YOUR WINDOW . BAY . BE . I CAN SEE IT . WATCH IT . ONE MORE
TIME . YOU WAKE UP . WITH A HEART ON . YOU HEAR THE MUSIC . OF
AN OLD DOG . WITH HER SOUL ON . TEAR OPEN THE WINDOW . STICK
YOUR FACE IN THE SNOW . HOW BEAUTIFUL YOU ARE . JOHN GREED . I
GASP . WHAT MASTERY . YOU HAVE . JOHN GREED . I BLEED .
ROSE . YOU CRY . LIKE A BULL IN THE FIELD . AND A HORSE IN THE
MOUNTAIN . AND A BIRD . IN THE SKY . AND THROW ON YOUR BOMBER
JACKET LIKE A CAPE . ROSE . YOU SHINE . LIKE A BEACON . THROUGH
THE FIRE AND THE SMOKE . OF EVERY POUND OF BURNING SHIT I'VE
EATEN . I CAN SEE IT . WATCH IT . ONE MORE TIME . YOU GRAB ME .
LIKE A PILLOW FULL OF DUCK DOWN . YES IT IS . IT'S ME . IT'S YOUR
DOG ROSE . BABY . IT'S ALRIGHT NOW . DON'T YOU FRET NOW . DON'T
YOU SWEAT NOW . ONE MORE TIME NOW . WHISPER TO ME . GOOD
DOG . BABY . ONE MORE TIME NOW . CARRY ME . BABY . UP THE
STAIRS TO HEAVEN . BABY . I'LL COME TO YOU . LIKE A GOLDEN
RETREIVER . OUT OF A GOLDEN STREAM . I BROUGHT YOU MY CHERRY .
BABY . NOW I BRING YOU MY DEAD DUCK . WHO GIVES A FUCK ..

NOW TELL ME TRULY . COULD YOU CUT THAT . COME ON . JOHN
CONFESS . FILMMAKER TO FILMMAKER . WOULD YOU CUT THAT . FOR
REASONS OF AESTHETICS .

OF COURSE NOT . SILLY . WE'RE A WELL KNOWN HYPE . JOHN . WE'RE
A BRAND NAME . WE DON'T WANT OUR TUNA WITH GOOD TASTE . WHEN
IT COULD TASTE SO GOOD . BABY . AND WHEN WE KNOW . IT'LL GO . A
QUESTION OF SIX DAYS .

AND THAT'S THE WAY . WE GO . ON . MISSING . THE POINT . BABY .
ONE MORE TIME . LEARNING TO LOVE . NOT LEARNING . TO LOVE
LOSING . BABY . OH YEAH . LEARNING . TO TRANSMUTE . LOSS TO
GAIN . BABY . COME ON . ARE YOU INSANE . YOU COME BACK . SOUL
SAFE . HAVING DONE YOUR TOOL . YOU LUCKY FOOL . DONE IT TO
DEATH . AND ONE MORE TIME . COME BACK ALIVE . SUCH JIVE . TO
WORK SOME MORE ON DYING . BABY . ONE MORE TIME . YOU'RE LYING

BYE BYE BABY . THERE YOU GO . AND NOBODY KNOWS . AND ALL IS
COOL . AND ALL IS WHITE . AND SILENT NIGHT . AND ALL YOU GOT TO
DO IS HOLD TIGHT . RIGHT .

JACK SMACK . I HEAR YOU KNOCKING . BUT YOU CAN'T COME IN . SING
ME A CHORUS OF CHERRY PIE . WRONG LIFE BABY . NEXT TIME .
MAYBE . I TELL YOU THE TRUTH . ONLY SLEEPING DOGS LIE .

Lee Breuer began his career as a director for the San Francisco Actor's Workshop in the early 1960s. After studying with the Berliner Ensemble and the Polish Laboratory Theatre he worked in France and Great Britain. Lee Breuer was one of the founding members of Mabou Mines in 1970, and has written and directed for the company THE RED HORSE, B.BEAVER and SHAGGY DOG ANIMATIONS. The SHAGGY DOG ANIMATION received an Obie Award as Best Play for 1977-78. He also directed for Mabou Mines the award-winning productions of Samuel Beckett's PLAY, COME AND GO, and THE LOST ONES. Lee Breuer is currently a Lecturer in Acting and Directing at the Yale School of Drama. He was awarded a Guggenheim Fellowship for 1977.

Frederic Ohringer

The ANIMATIONS were written for and produced by Mabou Mines in the decade 1968-78. Each was first shown in progress at the Paula Cooper Gallery in New York City and subsequently mounted in collaboration with Ellen Stewart-La Mama Experimental Theatre Club for THE RED HORSE ANIMATION and THE B.BEAVER ANIMATION; and Joseph Papp-New York Shakespeare Festival for THE SHAGGY DOG ANIMATION.

PHOTOS

Tom Berthiaume: 40, 51, 64; Benjamin Blackwell: 51; Bernard Burger: 155; Jaime Caro: 32, 44, 46, 47, 52, 53; L.B. Dallas: 99; Bill Davis: 65; Edit deAk: 64, 65, 70; Johan Elbers: 81, 82, 85, 94, 98, 100, 104, 111, 135, 143; Donna Gray: 85, 100, 107, 114, 136, 140, 144; Ken Kobland: 82, 87, 93, 96, 97, 115, 131; Richard Landry: 42; Babette Mangolte: 41, 58, 62, 63, 64, 65, 66, 67, 70; Kathy McHale: 60, 68, 71; Peter Moore: 45, 48; Ammon Nomis: 41, 49; David Stark: 86; Robin Thomas: 105.

PERFORMING ARTS JOURNAL PUBLICATIONS

"New Strategies for a New Sensibility"

PERFORMING ARTS JOURNAL PLAYSCRIPT SERIES

Also available:

THEATRE OF THE RIDICULOUS
The Magic Show of Dr. Ma-Gico by Kenneth Bernard
Stage Blood by Charles Ludlam
The Life of Lady Godiva by Ronald Tavel
Price: $4.95 (pbk); $9.95 (hbk)

THE RED ROBINS by Kenneth Koch
Price: $3.95 (pbk); $7.95 (hbk)

Other publications:

PERFORMING ARTS JOURNAL

PERFORMANCE ART MAGAZINE

Performing Arts Journal Publications
P.O. Box 858
Peter Stuyvesant Station
New York, N.Y. 10009